WEMBLEY SPEEDWAY

THE PRE-WAR YEARS

WEMBLEY SPEEDWAY
THE PRE-WAR YEARS

NORMAN JACOBS
& PETER LIPSCOMBE

TEMPUS

First published 2005

Tempus Publishing Limited
The Mill, Brimscombe Port,
Stroud, Gloucestershire, GL5 2QG
www.tempus-publishing.com

British Library Cataloguing in Publication Data.
A catalogue record for this book is available from the British Library.

ISBN 0 7524 3750 X

Typesetting and origination by Tempus Publishing Limited
Printed in Great Britain

CONTENTS

INTRODUCTION AND ACKNOWLEDGEMENTS

The most glamorous name in British sport is Wembley. When the Empire Stadium took up the sport speedway in 1929 it gave an air of respectability and helped bring it into the mainstream.

With Sir Arthur Elvin, 'Mr Wembley', at the helm everyone knew that it was in responsible hands and that here was a sport the whole family could enjoy. After all, Elvin was a very prim and proper person and he would not allow anything remotely disreputable to sully the sport he had personally invited into his stadium. During the 1930s one of his team's leading riders was universally known as 'Ginger' Lees but Elvin was so proper that he refused to allow the soubriquet 'Ginger' to be used before the name of Lees in his programmes, insisting that his initials, H.R., be used instead.

The other side to Elvin, however, was that he only wanted the best. He knew that Wembley Stadium was the best stadium in Great Britain and he wanted a team to go with it. His continual encouragement for his managers and riders was second to none and, in the early stages at least, his wishes were fulfilled as Wembley became the first 'big name' in the sport. Towards the middle of the 1930s it is true to say they suffered something of a setback and were overtaken by Belle Vue as the leading team in speedway, but Elvin never gave up and neither did his manager, Alec Jackson, who shared the dream of matching the Wembley team to its surroundings.

Jackson's policy of finding and developing youngsters was to pay many dividends after the Second World War, when Wembley dominated the British speedway scene from 1946 to 1953, winning the league seven times out of eight. In fact, the only year they lost it was 1948, when Elvin achieved his ambition of holding the Olympic Games at Wembley Stadium, forcing his speedway team to use Wimbledon as their home track for most of the season. There is no doubt the foundations of that success were laid before the Second World War. Jackson refined his methods of coaching, training and ways of looking after machinery so that when hostilities ended he was ready to take the speedway world by storm. At least two of the riders that came to dominate that peerless post-war team were pre-war Jackson discoveries, Tommy Price and George Wilks. This book is the story of those early years, the triumphs and despair of the pre-war Lions and the way those foundations for later success were laid.

There are also the individual stories, such as Frank Charles's 1935 Star Championship win, only to be followed four years later by his tragic death and, of course, the biggest story of them all, the Lions' captain Lionel Van Praag becoming the first-ever World Champion.

The authors would like to thank several people for their help in preparing this book by providing either photographs or information, or both. In particular they would like to thank Allen Trump, Ian Moultry, Ross Garrigan, Ken Taylor, John Chaplin, Mike Kemp and Jim Henry.

A brief explanation regarding the individual riders' calculated match averages (cmas) used throughout this book is required. Although in 1929 and 1933 the scoring system was 4-2-1 and up to and including 1934 all riders had a maximum of three rides per match, all cmas (unless otherwise specifically stated) are based on four rides per match with a 3-2-1 scoring system so as to give meaningful comparisons. The authord are grateful to Peter Jackson and Bob Ozanne for their help with the statistics.

ONE

HOW IT ALL BEGAN

In 1880 London's first underground railway company, the Metropolitan Railway Company, extended its line from Willesden Green to Harrow-on-the-Hill. The route took it through a small rural village set deep in the countryside among rolling hills. The name of this village was Wembley. Nearby was Wembley Park Leisure Grounds, which consisted of football and cricket pitches, a running track, fountains and waterfalls, walkways and flowerbeds. In 1889, in a bid to encourage more people to use his railway, the chairman of the railway company, Sir Edward Watkin, thought up the idea of building a big tourist attraction on the site. His chosen project was a tower to rival and beat Paris's Eiffel Tower. The builders went to work. The foundations were put into place and steel was erected. Unfortunately the building was taking shape on marshlands and, after completion of the first stage, it was discovered that the weight of the steel had caused the foundations to move and the base of the tower to tilt at an alarming angle. Sir Edward, in his disappointment, could not face the task of pulling down and rebuilding the tower, so he just abandoned the whole project leaving the leaning tower, which became known as 'Watkin's Folly', overlooking the leisure grounds, where it became a curious tourist attraction in its own right until it was dynamited out of existence in 1907.

Lord Strathcona had first put forward the idea of a British Empire Exhibition in 1913. Following the First World War (1914-1918) the idea gained the support of the Prime Minister, David Lloyd George, as a means of acknowledging the way that the British Empire had pulled together during the war. The Prince of Wales agreed to act as president of the committee set up to oversee the exhibition and, on 7 June 1920, at The Mansion House, he announced that his father, HM King George V, would become patron of the exhibition. By this time the government hadagreed to award a grant of £100,000 provided a further £500,000 could be raised from other sources. As part of the new complex a grand new sports arena was also to be built. The Wembley Park Leisure Ground, which by then had evolved into an eighteen-hole golf course, was selected as the ideal site. The exhibition area covered 219 acres and the area on which Watkin's Folly had once stood was chosen as the site for the new stadium. The Empire Stadium, as it was originally known, was built by architects Sir John Simpson and Maxwell Ayerton and the engineer Sir Owen Williams.

The first turf was cut on 10 January by HRH the Duke of York (later to become King George VI) and building work began. The intention was to make Wembley the finest sports stadium in the

The entrance to Wembley Stadium.

world. The dimensions were impressive – 890 feet long, 650 feet wide and the height from ground level to the top of the twin towers that adorned the stadium was 76 feet. Over 250,000 tons of earth and clay were moved to level the site, 25,000 tons of ferro-concrete were used, 1,400 tons of structural steel, 1,000 tons of reinforced steel and over half a million rivets. The stadium was designed to house 100,000 people with 23,000 seated. Yet without the use of great cranes or massive concrete mixers this stadium was built in just 300 working days, at a cost of £750,000. A whole battalion of infantry marked time in the stadium to see if it would stand up to the test of vibrations.

When it was opened in 1923, the centre green was surrounded by a quarter-mile running track, with a 220-yard straight track, the first in Europe. Wembley Stadium opened with the FA Cup final between West Ham and Bolton on 28 April 1923, with Bolton winning 2-0. At one o'clock the official attendance was 126,047. Three-quarters of an hour later, the gates were shut but, with over 150,000 outside the stadium, people pushed and swarmed over the turnstiles and barriers. Nothing was going to stop them seeing this final. It was only thanks to the policeman on his white horse pushing the crowds back that the final ever took place. The image of that lone policeman, a reservist by the name of George Scorey, is now enshrined forever in the annals of sporting history.

The Empire Exhibition itself was a remarkable event, with fountains, lakes, gardens and many pavilions, each representing the architectural style of the countries exhibiting. It was opened by King George V on 23 April 1924, and was an immediate success. So successful was it, in fact, that it reopened between May and October the following year, lifting the final attendance to 27,102,498. There were 4,500,000 admissions to the Empire Stadium alone.

And so to Arthur Elvin, later to be known as 'Mr Wembley'. Elvin was born on 5 July 1899 in Norwich. He left school at the age of fourteen and took a number of jobs before joining the Royal Flying Corps during the First World War. He was shot down over France and spent two years in a prisoner of war camp.

A general view of the British Empire Exhibition.

In 1924, Elvin was once again looking for a job and was offered employment at the British Empire Exhibition as an assistant in a cigarette kiosk at £4 10s a week. He took the job and during his spare time he walked all round the exhibition grounds getting to know them like the backs of his hands. The following year, with the knowledge he had gained from his year as a sales assistant, he decided to take the plunge and bought his own shop. Being the ambitious sort, he didn't stop at just one shop, but bought a total of eight on the grounds in time for the 1925 exhibition season. The cost was £100. Elvin kept his shops open later than most and in this way he was able to take more money. With a profit margin of around ten per cent for each shop, he was able to make £1,000 clear profit by the time the exhibition closed in October 1925. It was while running his shops that he met his future wife, the manageress of the jewellery section in the Palace of Industry.

After the end of the exhibition a buildings entrepreneur by the name of Jimmy White bought the grounds for £350,000, while the versatile Elvin assumed the role of demolition contractor and made his fortune by buying up the derelict pavilions one by one from White, demolishing them and selling off the scrap materials. Elvin then offered White £122,500 for the stadium, £12,000 down with the balance plus interest to be paid over the next ten years.

Unfortunately, White committed suicide still owing £270,000 for the original purchase. Elvin now found that if he wanted the stadium he would have to find the rest of the purchase price of the whole site within fourteen days or he would lose the £12,000 he had already paid. Fortunately a new company, the Wembley Company, with capital of £230,000, stepped in and bought the site. At 6.30 p.m. on 17 August 1927, the company honoured Elvin's original offer and sold the stadium to him for the original offer price of £122,500. At 6.31 p.m. on 17 August 1927, the new company bought the stadium back from Elvin for £150,000, Elvin took his profits in shares, becoming the largest shareholder. He was then appointed managing director of the newly named Wembley Stadium and Greyhound Racecourse Limited. Not a bad minute's work and one that was to have a wide and beneficial impact on the sport, as yet unknown in Great Britain – speedway.

TWO

1929 – SPEEDWAY ARRIVES

By 1929 Elvin had discovered a new sport, a sport that had taken Britain by storm and was attracting both young and old in this age of fast machines. The sport in question was, of course, speedway and with league racing about to start, Elvin announced that Wembley would join the new Southern League. Johnnie S. Hoskins, the pioneering Australian promoter, was brought in as manager and a new track was laid at a cost of some £250,000.

A special badge in silver was commissioned by Arthur Elvin to celebrate the opening of Wembley Speedway. This souvenir was presented to all the riders at that first meeting. The badge showed the twin towers of the stadium in white, with a blue sky above and the words 'Wembley Speedway' written across the top. Below was a silver bar with the inscription, 'Rider at the first speedway meeting held at the Wembley Stadium May 16 1929'. Just thirty of these badges were made. In fact, it was originally intended that Wembley's colours would be blue and white, but Hoskins realised that this clashed with Stamford Bridge, so he changed them to red and white.

At that first meeting on 16 May 1929, two trophies, a silver shield and a silver cup, to become the absolute property of the winners, were contested. *Auto* magazine stated that the organisation at this first meeting was excellent, with the track being in first-class condition. An International Match Race series between the Australian Billy Lamont and the Englishman Roger Frogley was won 2-0 by the Englishman, with a fastest time of 83.8 seconds. Also on the programme was a trophy called 'The Cinders'. The cinders in question were taken from the surface of the actual track and then enclosed in a silver urn. This trophy was awarded to the holder of the one-lap track record. The first winner was the American Ray Tauser, who recorded 21 seconds, or 36.82mph, just beating the English star Buster Frogley, Roger's brother, who lapped in 21.2 seconds. The Silver Shield was won by Roger Frogley in a time of 83.8 seconds, 36.94mph.

The following evening Wembley rode its first league match at London's White City. At that time a league match was just six heats. The Wembley team for that historic match consisted of Buster Frogley (captain), Charlie Briggs, Nobby Key, Crawley Rous, Len Reeve, Bert Fairweather and Ben Hieatt. The scoring was four points for a win, two points for second and one point for third. The full results of Wembley's first-ever league match were as follows:

Left: Only thirty of these blue and white badges were made and given to the riders at the first meeting. This is Billy Lamont's badge and says: 'Billy Lamont Rider at the first speedway meeting held at the Wembley Stadium May 16 1929'.

Below: The Wembley team, 1929. From left to right: Jack Jackson, Jack Ormston, Johnnie Hoskins (manager), Buster Frogley, Harry Whitfield, Bert Fairweather, Len Reeve.

HEAT 1

1st	CLEM CORT	WHITE CITY	84.6 seconds
2nd	BUSTER FROGLEY	WEMBLEY	
3rd	JACK BISHOP	WHITE CITY	

HEAT 2

1st	BERT FAIRWEATHER	WEMBLEY	90.2 seconds
2nd	DEL FOSTER	WHITE CITY	
3rd	HAROLD CROOK	WHITE CITY	

HEAT 3

1st	HILARY BUCHANAN	WHITE CITY	87.8 seconds
2nd	CRAWLEY ROUS	WEMBLEY	
3rd	EDDIE GREEN	WHITE CITY	

HEAT 4

1st	CLEM CORT	WHITE CITY	85.4 seconds
2nd	BERT FAIRWEATHER	WEMBLEY	
3rd	CHARLIE BRIGGS	WEMBLEY	

HEAT 5

1st	DEL FOSTER	WHITE CITY	90.6 seconds
2nd	HAROLD CROOK	WHITE CITY	
3rd	NOBBY KEY	WEMBLEY	

HEAT 6

1st	BUSTER FROGLEY	WEMBLEY	not available
2nd	EDDIE GREEN	WHITE CITY	
3rd	LEN REEVE	WEMBLEY	

WHITE CITY 25   WEMBLEY 17

The pay structure at this time was 15s a point, hence the first man received £3, the second £1 10s and the third 15s. In the early days most speedway tracks opened twice a week. Wembley was no exception, racing on Tuesday and Thursday nights.

Wembley's first league match at the Empire Stadium took place on Tuesday 21 May against West Ham, and resulted in a win for the Lions by 29 points to 12. The following evening, Wednesday 22 May, Wembley travelled to Stamford Bridge and were beaten out of sight by a powerful Bridge team. The score was Stamford Bridge 33 Wembley 9. The return the following Tuesday, 28 May, was not much better as the Lions went down by 10 points, Wembley 16 Stamford Bridge 26. Only Bert Fairweather and Buster Frogley won a heat for the home side.

At this time another Aussie speed merchant, Stan Catlett, had worked his passage over here as an engineer on the SS *Treginnin*. On his arrival he was immediately signed up by Hoskins and rode his first race for Wembley against Coventry at the Brandon track. It had been a rush getting there on time and he arrived without his riding boots. It appears a spare left boot was available, while Bert Fairweather and Coventry's Jack Parker took it in turns to lend him a right boot. The meeting took place on 1 June and saw the Lions lose by 13 points, Wembley 14 Coventry 27. After this somewhat rushed start, Catlett soon began to make a name for himself. At Nottingham he won the Silver Cup by beating local champion George Wigfield in two straight heats. He then motored over to Leicester on the same evening and accounted for northern star Sherlock in a thrilling match race. After this he said, 'I earned more money in half an hour than I received for three months' hard work aboard the ship coming over.'

Early in June, with the success of league racing assured, it was decided in the interest of the fans to increase matches from six heats to nine, which meant the total number of points to be competed for rose to 63. This new arrangement had no effect on matches already raced and the number of points scored by the respective teams would still stand to their credit. Wembley rode at the Custom House track on 13 June under this new arrangement and won an exciting meeting by one point, 32-31.

On 4 July, it was Wembley's turn to stage their round of the 'Star Championship'. As the popularity of speedway throughout the country grew, the newspapers began to take speedway to their hearts. The proprietors of the *Star* decided to approach the Motor Cycle Track Racing promoters with regard to launching a new competition to find the best riders in the country and presented two trophies, one for overseas riders and the other for English riders. Both trophies were to be known as the Star Trophy. The competition was run on a match race knock-out principle. So as to make the competition fair to both riders a match race series of the best of three heats took place on the home track of each competitor. Each track nominated one overseas rider and one English rider to take part. The home riders nominated were Gus Kuhn (Stamford Bridge), Roger Frogley (Crystal Palace), Colin Watson (London White City), Eric Spencer (Harringay), Jack Parker (Brandon, Coventry), Jimmy Haynes (Southampton), Ivor Creek (West Ham), Tommy Croombs (Lea Bridge), Jim Kempster (Wimbledon) and Buster Frogley (Wembley). The foreign riders were Frank Arthur (Harringay), Stan Catlett (Wembley), Alf Chick (Coventry), Billy Galloway (Southampton), Max Grosskreutz (Lea Bridge), Vic Huxley (Wimbledon), Ron Johnson (Crystal Palace), Billy Lamont (London White City), Sprouts Elder (West Ham) and Art Pechar (Stamford Bridge). The winner of each final would receive £100 in cash plus the trophy, which had a value of £25.

The first round took place at Southampton with the Australian Billy Galloway riding against the American Sprouts Elder. Galloway, lacking the speed, was beaten in two straight runs and so a new event was born, an event that, seven years later, was to father the World Speedway Championship. The meeting at Wembley on 4 July saw Australian and home favourite Stan Catlett defeat Coventry's Alf Chick 2-0.

By 16 July the league table looked like this:

Southern League Table

	Matches	Won	Lost	For	Against	Points
Stamford Bridge	10	10	0	389	157	20
Southampton	10	9	1	316	219	18

West Ham	10	5	5	277	216	10
Perry Bar	11	5	6	266.5	313.5	10
Coventry	6	4	2	160	152	8
Crystal Palace	9	4	5	235	226	8
Wimbledon	10	4	6	240	304	8
Lea Bridge	10	4	6	242	281	8
White City	8	3	5	203	235	6
Harringay	9	2	7	206.5	299.5	4
Wembley	11	2	9	233	352	4

Wembley had made a disastrous start to the season, losing nine of their first eleven fixtures. This was due mainly to the fact that by the time Wembley had put in its application to join the league the best riders had already been signed up by the other teams. The average attendance for the first six home meetings was a poor 2,786. Something had to be done or Wembley would sink under heavy financial losses of £500 per meeting. The first decision made by the Wembley management was to limit racing to just once a week, on Thursday nights. Elvin then told Hoskins to scour the country for new talent to make the team more competitive. Hoskins travelled thousands of miles looking to sign up riders to join the team. His first signing was Harry Whitfield, a star rider with Middlesbrough. Whitfield also told Hoskins about a young lad he knew who was racing at Whitley Bay and Middlesbrough. The lad in question was Jack Ormston, who was just nineteen years old. He had very little experience of cinder tracks as he raced mainly on sand and grass tracks. Hoskins, desperate for new talent, signed him up. He was an instant success and accomplished one of the finest performances ever seen in speedway when, after just fourteen rides, he lowered the track record at Newcastle. He followed up this achievement seven days later by breaking the track record in the Imperial Handicap at his new home track, Wembley. He clocked 89.6 seconds, beating his friend Harry Whitfield's standing-start record by 0.4 seconds.

In spite of these moves, disaster was near. The other tracks did not want Wembley in the league because gate receipts were so poor. With bankruptcy and closure staring him in the face, Elvin then had a brilliant idea. Football and cricket teams had supporters' clubs. Why not speedway? By joining the Wembley Speedway Supporters' Club a small concession would be given on the entrance fee with a number of other benefits available. Elvin's brainwave proved to be Wembley's salvation. People joined the supporters' club in droves. Badges were produced, riders' photographs sold and red and white scarves introduced – merchandise as we know it today had moved in. So successful did Wembley now become that other tracks took up the idea, but Wembley continued to dominate. Instead of empty seats, the crowds increased from 2,000 to 19,000. Wembley Lions had arrived and Thursday nights would never be the same again.

Unfortunately, just as things were beginning to look up, Wembley suffered from a number of injuries. The eighteen-year-old Bert Fairweather broke his collarbone after a mix-up with Wally Lloyd, while at the same time Harry Whitfield began to suffer from a groggy knee. Following these injuries, Art Warren was promoted to the team.

Wembley's next big event was the Speedway Derby held on 25 July, the finalists being Roger Frogley of Crystal Palace, the High Beech star Jack Barnett, young Jack Ormston and Wembley's captain Buster Frogley. Speedway fans were treated to a battle royal between the two Jacks, which was eventually won by Ormston in the best time of the evening, 85 seconds or 36.41mph.

Buster Frogley, Wembley's first captain.

On the same bill, races for the home riders in the Star Championship took place between Buster Frogley and Wimbledon's 'Smiling' Jim Kempster. Frogley won in two straight runs with plenty to spare.

In the meantime, the Lions' fortunes had changed from losing to winning. On 18 July Wembley rode and beat the Lea Bridge team at the Empire Stadium by 41 points to 21 and, some thirteen days later, they won the return by three points at the Lea Bridge track. There was no stopping the Lions now and they won their seven remaining league fixtures. Wembley were at last riding as a team, led by their captain Buster Frogley with the brilliant Jack Ormston, Aussie Stan Catlett, Bert Fairweather, Jack Jackson and Ron Hieatt to back him up.

However, injuries continued to occur. Harry Whitfield sustained further damage to his knee and Ormston suffered a fractured collarbone after winning the Speedway Derby but, as Ormston's injury occurred, Whitfield made his return to the team. Arthur Elvin was worried about the fitness of his riders and had a gymnasium put into the stadium. He also brought in a trainer. Each week the riders underwent a strict training routine as fitness was essential in this fast-moving sport. For Wembley, professionalism had arrived.

At this time Wembley put out a challenge to race any team in the country. The first team to accept was Newcastle on 15 August. Newcastle were a strong team with the brilliant Gordon Byers and the Creasor brothers, Fred and Walter. The Lions won by 16 points to 12. Also included in the Newcastle team was the world's tallest rider, Wally Huntley, who stood 6ft 9ins. He was put into a match race against the brilliant little Wally Lloyd, star of the Perry Barr team. Lloyd stood a mere 5ft 4ins. The smaller Wally won at a canter.

After that, Wembley raced challenge matches against many teams, particularly in Scotland and the North of England, including Edinburgh, Glasgow, Barnsley, Leeds and Middlesbrough.

Hoskins was able to use these matches to gauge the strength of the opposition riders and any who looked likely to make the grade he offered a place in the Lions set-up.

One of his own riders who had ridden particularly well in the north was Harry Whitfield, who was known as '£100 Harry' in Scotland because, on 27 June, he won the Glasgow White City Open Championship, on 28 June he won the Scottish Championship at the Marine Gardens, Edinburgh and on 26 July he won the Marine Gardens Track Championship, each of which carried a prize of £100.

Some interesting statistics on the Lions' team demonstrate the remarkable consistency of its riders. Buster Frogley had ridden 84 rides and won exactly half of them, but it was Wembley junior Art Warren who had the biggest percentage of wins to his credit since his victory in the novice event back in June.

	No. of rides	First	Second	Percentage no. of wins
Art Warren	16	10	2	62.5
Buster Frogley	84	42	19	50.0
Bert Fairweather	43	21	10	48.9
Stan Catlett	29	12	7	41.4

On Thursday 29 August Miss Eva Asquith beat Miss Sunny Somerset in a match race, the attendance being an amazing 41,000. Previous to this, on 4 June, Eva had beaten Fay Taylour 2-0. Also on the programme was the second round of the Star Championship. Colin Watson, star of London's White City, beat Buster Frogley in two straight runs. He shattered the track record in one race, clocking 82.4 seconds and winning by nearly six clear lengths.

The other second round results saw Roger Frogley beating Ivor Creek while Jack Parker was given a bye. In the Overseas section, Sprouts Elder of West Ham lost to Wimbledon's Vic Huxley and Frank Arthur of Harringay defeated White City's Billy Lamont. Following his victory over Alf Chick, Catlett had had to withdraw from the competition as he had returned to Australia. This meant that the two Queensland riders, Huxley and Arthur, had qualified for the Overseas Star final.

Back at the Lions' den on 12 September over 49,000 people teemed into the Empire Stadium to see Wembley beat Southampton in a £100 challenge match by 19 points to 9. By this time over 10,000 people had joined the supporters' club and gates were improving week upon week. Wembley was now becoming the Mecca of big events. Other tracks were trying to copy them, but there was nothing bigger than the £500 challenge match against the league champions from Stamford Bridge, led by Gus Kuhn.

According to reports, over 60,000 fans poured in to the stadium that night cheering wildly for the Lions. Wembley won every heat except one, which was won by Gus Kuhn. Buster Frogley and Harry Whitfield won three races each, Jack Ormston two and the Lions won by 19 points. The final score was Wembley 41 The Bridge 22.

Some two days later the return match took place at Stamford Bridge with another huge crowd. All seats and programmes were sold out. The Bridge team were not to be beaten on their own track. The Wembley team had to struggle with machine failures and were beaten by 42 points to 20, which, when added to the previous score, made a total of 64 points to Stamford Bridge and 61 points to Wembley.

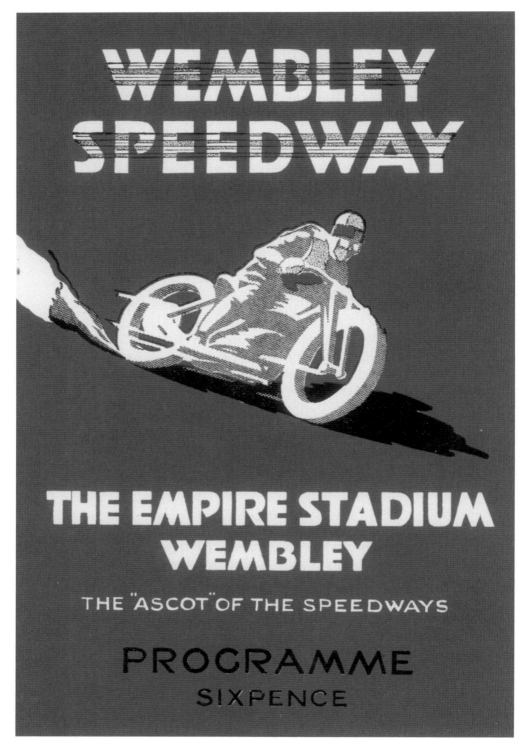

A programme cover from the meeting held on 14 November 1929, 'The Wembley Track Championship'.

Wembley's season ran into late November, the last meeting being held on 28 November with an all-star field of Rochdale's Squib Burton, Colin Watson of London's White City, Cliff Watson of Salford, Newcastle's Walter Creasor, Tommy Price of Liverpool, Triss Sharp of Crystal Palace, Gosforth's P.F. Parker, Wally Lloyd of Perry Barr and Alf Foulds of Lea Bridge plus the Lions' favourites, captain Buster Frogley, Harry Whitfield and the new November signing, former Leeds star Arthur Atkinson.

They were all riding for the Silver Cup, a trophy presented by the Wembley Stadium caterers. The winner was Wembley's own Harry Whitfield, runner-up was Walter Creasor and third was Arthur Atkinson.

So ended the first season at Wembley. It had started back in May with an opening attendance of some 4,500 people (this later dropped to under 2,000) but ended the season with over 60,000 fans for the derby match against Stamford Bridge. Also in this first year, on 7 November, the BBC had made one of its first outside broadcasts covering the sport with Wembley manager Johnnie Hoskins proving his versatility by acting as commentator.

Wembley had now become the most popular track in the country and the Lions' roar was heard everywhere at the mention of Wembley Speedway. Jack Ormston, the Wembley star in that first year, had done so well that he was able to buy a Bugatti car – he already owned a two-seater Tiger Moth aeroplane. At the end of the season, he travelled to Australia for a season's racing Down Under.

During the winter, monthly dances were held on a Thursday night at Wembley Stadium. This was another of Elvin's ideas to keep the supporters happy during the close season. In fact, the dances were so popular that you had to book your ticket well in advance and the only way to do that was through the supporters' club. Wembley's own Buster Frogley was an expert saxophonist and led his own band that, naturally, made regular appearances at the stadium dances. A permanent licence was issued to the stadium restaurant to allow alcoholic refreshment to be sold until 11.30 p.m.

1929 League Averages – qualification 6 matches

	Matches	Rides	Points	CMA
Jack Ormston	7	19	53	11.16
Buster Frogley	18	51	138	10.82
Stan Catlett	8	23	54	9.39
Bert Fairweather	12	31	59	7.61
Len Reeve	15	39	67	6.87
Ron Hieatt	12	33	50	6.06
Jack Jackson	14	40	54	5.40
Vic Deale	8	18	18	4.00
Crawley Rous	9	22	17	3.09

Southern League Results

Date	H/A	Opponents	W/L/D	Score
17 May	Home	White City	Lost	17-25
21 May	Home	West Ham	Won	29-12
22 May	Away	Stamford Bridge	Lost	9-33
29 May	Home	Stamford Bridge	Lost	16-26
1 June	Away	Coventry	Lost	14-27
13 June	Away	West Ham	Won	32-31
18 June	Home	Harringay	Lost	31-32
19 June	Away	Southampton	Lost	20-43
4 July	Home	Crystal Palace	Lost	23-40
11 July	Home	Southampton	Lost	22-40
13 July	Away	Crystal Palace	Lost	21-42
18 July	Home	Lea Bridge	Won	41-21
31 July	Away	Lea Bridge	Won	33-30
1 August	Home	Coventry	Won	36-27
8 August	Home	Wimbledon	Won	48-15
12 August	Away	Wimbledon	Won	36-27
17 August	Away	Perry Barr	Won	33-30
5 September	Home	Perry Barr	Won	42-21
19 September	Home	White City	Won	39-24
28 September	Away	Harringay	Won	38-25

Final League Table

	Raced	Won	Lost	For	Against	Points
Stamford Bridge	20	17	3	767	408	34
Southampton	20	16	4	672	501	32
Coventry	20	14	6	658	534	28
Crystal Palace	20	11	9	584	568	22
WEMBLEY	20	11	9	580	571	22
West Ham	20	8	12	539	612	16
White City	20	8	12	543	651	16
Harringay	20	7	13	538	553	14
Perry Barr	20	7	13	499	650	14
Lea Bridge	20	6	14	550	599	12
Wimbledon	20	5	15	495	679	10

NO. 1 – COLIN WATSON

Colin Watson was born in Ilford in 1899 and was one of the country's top motor cyclists in both trials and road racing before taking part in Britain's first-ever speedway meeting at High Beech on 19 February 1928 on his Harley Pea-Shooter. In his first race on the dirt track he took on the experienced Australian Billy Galloway and very nearly beat him, just being passed on the last lap.

He followed up his debut by racing at a number of London tracks as they began opening up in 1928. He was spotted by leading Australian star Frank Arthur, who took him under his wing, training him, managing him and making sure he had the best equipment available.

When league racing came along in 1929, Watson was signed up by London White City, moving to Harringay at the start of the 1930 season. Shortly after the start of the season he shocked the Harringay management by putting in a transfer request. A £100 fee was placed on him and it was Wembley who came up with the money. Although Stamford Bridge had wanted to sign him, they refused Harringay's asking price as they considered it too much. This was to be the start of a bitter rivalry between Wembley and Stamford Bridge, with Watson very much the man in the middle and he became both hero and villain, depending on which set of supporters you belonged to.

He was immensely popular with his own fans and his own riders and when Buster Frogley relinquished the captaincy of the Lions, Watson was the unanimous choice to take over. At Stamford Bridge, however, he was booed and jeered whenever he appeared. On one particular occasion a Stamford Bridge rider fell while racing against Watson. The Bridge supporters thought Watson had knocked him off and he was bombarded with broken bottles, orange peel and anything else that came to hand.

When the British Individual Match Race Championship was first introduced, the great Vic Huxley was nominated as champion. Chosen as his first challenger was Colin Watson. It was a mark of the esteem in which he was held throughout Britain (except maybe at Stamford Bridge!) and of his riding ability.

Watson led Wembley to many successes and was a star at whichever track he rode on except Wimbledon. For some reason he could never get to grips with the Plough Lane track. In particular there was one spot on the track, just coming out of the pit bend, where he fell time after time. He claimed there was a bump there, though no other rider seemed to have the

Colin Watson.

trouble he had. 'Watson's bump' became famous and many people came to Wimbledon when he was riding just to see him fall at that spot!

Eventually the Wimbledon management decided to see if there was anything in Watson's claim that there was something wrong with the track at this point and decided to dig it up. The spades hadn't dug very far when, amazingly, the excavators found a full-sized surveyor's tripod buried in the track at the exact spot where Watson kept falling. But it was never really explained why it was only Watson who found this bump.

As the original pioneers gradually faded out of the sport, Watson continued, still producing racing of the very highest quality. At the start of the 1934 season he was the oldest rider still racing in the top flight and he started off the season dropping just six points from his first seven matches. Although his form faded a little after that stunning start, it was a bitter blow when, before the 1935 league season had even started, Watson broke his leg in a Best Pairs event. It was an injury that kept him out of the saddle for two years and when he did come back he was nothing like the rider he had once been. He transferred to West Ham in 1938 and was loaned out to Second Division Sheffield.

Watson astounded the speedway world not only by making a comeback for West Ham after the Second World War but by riding as if he'd never been out of the top echelon. In a team that included the likes of Eric Chitty, Malcolm Craven and Bob Harrison, Watson was able to comfortably hold down a heat leader position. He was forty-seven years old, the oldest rider still riding in the First Division and one of the few still clinging to the old leg-trailing style.

Watson's last meeting was on 13 July at Bradford. In a second-half scratch race he crashed and hit a lighting standard by the safety fence. He half fell from his machine, which dragged him head down for about twenty yards. He was rushed to hospital with a fractured skull and a punctured lung. His condition was described as critical and he lay unconscious for many days. Fortunately he did recover but he never rode again.

He rode nine times for England in official Test matches, scoring a total of 45 points. Because of his injury in 1935 he never qualified for a World Championship final.

THREE

1930 – SUCCESS

Arthur Elvin and his manager, Johnnie Hoskins, had done their homework well. New riders were signed up before the end of 1929; Arthur Atkinson had agreed terms the previous November, followed by Charlie Shelton of Nottingham and Leeds' star George Greenwood.

By January 1930, while other clubs were still formulating their ideas for a supporters' club, Elvin took the Wembley club a stage further. Being a very shrewd businessman he figured that he could double the attendance by going even further with the meeting entry concessions and halving the price of admission for club members, thereby maintaining profits. But this would have the added bonus of allowing the fans more money to spend on stadium items, thus increasing the cash flow into the stadium on race nights. The admission prices at that time were 1s 2d, 2s 4d, 5s and 10s, but for supporters' club members the prices would range from 7d to 5s. Inside the stadium, red and white berets were sold for 1s 6d each, scarves at 2s 6d, neckties at 6 ½d each, pennants at 1s 6d each, while the largest seller of all, the Wembley badge, was sold at 1s.

January saw a number of changes to the Southern League. A meeting of promoters confirmed that sixteen teams would take part, Coventry, Crystal Palace, Hall Green, Harringay, High Beech, Lea Bridge, Leicester Stadium, Nottingham, Perry Barr, Portsmouth, Southampton, Stamford Bridge, Wembley, West Ham, White City (London) and Wimbledon. However, before the season started, White City and Portsmouth withdrew.

The method of scoring was changed to the now familiar three points for a win, two points for second and one point for third.

Hoskins continued to sign up star names and in March the latest rider to join the ranks of the Lions was the New Zealand champion Wally Kilmister, holder of many track records Down Under. In the event, however, Kilmister did not arrive in this country until late May. His signing was followed by that of Middlesbrough captain Norman Evans, Terry White, also from Middlesbrough, Nottingham rider Tom Pidcock and Gosforth's Gus Mordue. One rider, Nobby Key, went in the opposite direction, being transferred to Nottingham. This left Wembley with twenty riders under contract – so many, in fact, that they decided to run two teams: the Lions, an all-English team captained by Buster Frogley, and the Cubs, captained by Aussie Stan Catlett.

Before Wembley opened their home season, their riders were already proving to be in good form as Arthur Atkinson won the Century Trophy at Lea Bridge and Charlie Shelton won the Golden Helmet at Cleveland Park, Middlesbrough.

Arthur Atkinson.

When the season did open for Wembley on 8 May it was in front of royalty in the person of Princess Arthur of Connaught. That night 40,000 cheering spectators saw the Lions dispose of Leicester 34-21 in a Southern League match, although the star rider of the night was Leicester's Syd Jackson, who scored a maximum. Over 2,000 badges were sold that evening and the management reported that the supporters' club now boasted 15,000 members.

The following week, on 15 May, both the Lions and the Cubs were in action. The Lions won away at Nottingham by 31 points to 22, partly because of Elvin's instruction to Hoskins that he should send a full team of mechanics to travel with the team on all away fixtures. To get to away fixtures, Harry Whitfield had purchased a new bright red Chevrolet van to transport himself and his bikes, with his own name and the legend 'Wembley Speedway' painted on the doors. Ormston had given up flying to away fixtures following a crash and was now travelling by car.

Back at the Empire Stadium the Cubs took on a team labelled the West of England. However, before the match started one of the leading female riders of the day, Mrs Billie Smith, fell during the grand parade. Because of this incident the Wembley management banned any further appearances by lady riders. Jessie Hole, later Jessie Ennis, was leading the parade. She told Peter Lipscombe in an interview many years later, 'The stadium was packed. I was in front of the other two [Mrs Billie Smith and Sunny Somerset] so I didn't see what happened because they were behind me, but I was told later that one of the boys cut across in front of Billie, she shut off and went over the handlebars, breaking her collarbone. It was then given out over the loudspeakers that the race [a special ladies' exhibition race] would not take place and at the end of the meeting they announced that the incident had been reported to the ACU [Auto Cycle

Union, the ruling body for speedway in this country], which eventually ruled that women were banned from ever taking part in dirt track racing in England again.'

This does seem to be a bit of overreaction on the part of the authorities, however the story behind the ban was reportedly that because of the nature of her injury the St John Ambulance men attending Mrs Smith had had to cut her clothes away on the track and it was felt improper to expose a lady to thousands of spectators in this way. Hence the complete ban to ensure it couldn't happen again.

After this incident, the Cubs went on to beat the West of England by 30 points to 24. Once again it was one of the opposition riders, Bill Clibbett, who was the star of the evening, though Norman Evans and Stan Catlett rode well for Wembley.

Hoskins had still not finished his signing spree, and he caused a big sensation when he signed up the Harringay star and one of the pioneers of the sport who had ridden at Britain's first recognised speedway meeting at High Beech, Colin Watson, for £100.

The evening of 29 May was a big occasion for Wembley with two new arrivals, the first being Johnnie Hoskins' five-year-old son Ian, who made his debut as the team mascot on a Fruin Special. This was another first for Wembley as they became the first team to have an official mascot. The second new arrival saw the long-awaited appearance of Wally Kilmister, riding for the Cubs. In the event the wait proved worthwhile as Kilmister scored a maximum in the Cubs' 41-10 annihilation of High Beech.

Speedway's first mascot, Johnnie Hoskins' five-year-old son Ian, seen here racing his dad around the Wembley track.

The battle of the giants took place at Stamford Bridge on 4 June as Wembley took on the league champions on their home track. Unfortunately for the Lions, George Greenwood was injured the night before and, although his replacement, Bert Fairweather, rode above himself, he could not prevent the Wembley team chalking up their first loss of the season, going down by five points.

Three days later in a special challenge match at the Empire Stadium, the Lions went down again, this time to their own Cubs team, to whom they lost 31-28.

At Wimbledon on 30 June the first official Test match between England and Australia took place in this country, with Australia winning by 35 points to 17. One Wembley rider was chosen to represent his country, Jack Ormston, who rode at number six for England. Unfortunately he did not have a good evening, riding well below form to finish with just one point from three rides, and that only because his teammate Jack Parker fell in front of him.

Four days later, on 3 July, one of the stars of the victorious Australian team, 'Cyclone' Billy Lamont, became the first rider to travel at over 40mph at Wembley when he took the one-lap record for the Cinders Trophy, knocking one-fifth of a second off the track record. That same day, the Cubs were in action at Southampton in a challenge match, being well and truly beaten by an in-form Saints team led by Geoff Taylor and the high-scoring Ernie Rickman.

Wembley beat West Ham at Custom House on 8 July. The match was remarkable for the fact that the Wembley heat leaders crossed the line first in every heat. Ormston and Watson scored nine each, but poor old Whitfield was disqualified in one race for 'looking round', so he was only credited with six points. The Lions won the match 33-21. The points gained from this match sent Wembley to the top of the league, having won eight out of their first nine matches.

On 12 July the eight London promoters met and agreed to introduce the London Cup to the speedway calendar. Elvin successfully argued that the format for these meetings should be sixteen heats with eight riders in each team. He knew he had better strength in depth than most other teams and thought the extra two riders would help the Lions. The new competition was to be run on a knock-out formula with results decided on aggregate points from home and away legs. The draw was held at the promoters meeting and saw Wembley drawn against High Beech, with the first leg to be held at the Empire Stadium on 7 August.

Later that same week, the ACU announced that the 1930 Star Riders' final would be held at Wembley on 12 September with twelve qualifying riders drawn in four heats, each heat having three riders. For the first time, Wembley had been recognised for the purpose of a major meeting; it was certainly not going to be the last.

A special challenge match race was held at the Empire Stadium on 18 July between the 'Great Dane' Morian Hansen, making his debut at Wembley, and the legendary American Sprouts Elder. Elder pushed out in front, but Hansen took him on the second lap by diving up the inside. Elder was forced wide to the fence and it looked as though the new Danish sensation had got the better of his American opponent, but unfortunately his bike slowed, allowing Elder to come back and snatch victory.

Thursday 26 July saw the Lions take on Hall Green in a particularly tough match. In each of the first four heats the finishes were so close that there was just half a wheel between first and second places. Unbelievably, heat five was even closer, as Wembley's Harry Whitfield and Hall Green ace Billy Dallison rode neck and neck round laps three and four with a dead heat the

£100 Harry – Harry Whitfield.

final result. With Harry Taft joining Dallison as a top performer that night, Hall Green really put the pressure on Wembley, who just scraped home by four points, the score being Lions 28.5 Hall Green 24.5.

Wembley also had one representative in the second Test match, this time Colin Watson, but he fared little better than Ormston had done. In his first race he collided with his partner, Jim Kempster, and fell; in his second he finished last and was replaced by Oliver Langton for the rest of the evening as he had not really recovered from his first-ride fall.

The following evening the Lions were up against a Lancashire team drawn from some of the best riders in the Northern League, captained by Eric Langton. The rest of the team was Cliff Watson, Ivor Creek, Max Grosskreutz, Norman Hartley, Wally Hull, Dusty Haigh and Chun Moore. Wembley, weakened by the absence of Colin Watson, still suffering from his fall the previous evening, and Jack Ormston, put up a great show considering the strength of the Northern riders and the loss of their own two top men. However, the main feature of the night was the riding of Eric Langton, who led his team to a four-point victory.

Following this meeting Buster Frogley resigned as Wembley captain, citing loss of form as his reason. Elvin and Hoskins agreed that the riders themselves should vote on who they wished to replace Frogley as captain and, at a specially convened meeting, Colin Watson was elected. George Greenwood took Frogley's place in the team.

There were a couple of controversial incidents in the away match at Plough Lane on 28 July, both involving Wimbledon's Billy Lamont. In heat three, Lamont was leading the race when the red lights came on due to a mechanical fault. The riders stopped and the race was re-run. In the re-run, Lamont fell and the Lions scored a 5-1.

Wembley's leading scorer in 1929 and 1930, Jack Ormston.

The second occurrence came in heat six. Watson and Atkinson were leading Lamont when Atkinson started to wobble and looked as though he was about to fall. Lamont, immediately behind him, laid his bike down to avoid hitting him, but Atkinson recovered and finished the race. Wimbledon protested that the race should have been stopped and re-run, but the steward dismissed their protest. Wembley went on to win 32-21.

The last day of July witnessed the Empire Stadium's biggest crowd of the season as approximately 50,000 spectators saw Vic Huxley take the Grand Prix individual trophy and £100. The final was a tragedy for Wembley's Stan Catlett, who got away from the start in first place but fell on the second bend and was hit by Jack Ormston. Catlett sustained a compound fracture of his left leg and his season was over. With no money coming in, Catlett took to autographing postcard photographs of himself in his hospital bed, raising over £30 in fourteen days.

The long-awaited first leg of the first round of the London Cup took place on 7 August and saw Wembley wipe the floor with High Beech, defeating them by 71 points to 25. So much interest had been aroused in the new competition that the London newspaper the *Evening News* had by now stepped in to sponsor it. Although the Lions were defeated in the second leg at the King's Oak track it was only by eight points, 52-44, so they went through to the semi-finals with an aggregate score of 115 to High Beech's 77.

Another major new competition was held on 30 August when Crystal Palace staged the London Riders' Championship, an individual title open to riders with London clubs. Twenty-seven of the capital's best took part, with the victor proving to be Wembley's Jack Ormston, who beat West Ham's Bluey Wilkinson in the final. Ormston received a £100 cheque and the 30 guinea trophy presented by the Maharajah of Tikari as well as, of course, the title of London Champion.

By the end of August Wembley had raced 20 matches, winning 17, drawing 1 and losing just 2. They were sitting on top of the Southern League with 35 points. Their great rivals, Stamford Bridge, were in second place eight points behind, having lost 6 of their 20 matches. However, there was a shock in store for the rampant Lions as, in their next home match on 4 September, Wembley went down to defeat by Stamford Bridge. The Pensioners' captain, Gus Kuhn, rode superbly, gaining a maximum and inspiring his team. The league title was back in the balance.

Another large crowd witnessed the Star Riders' final on 12 September. This was a night dominated by the two great Australian riders Vic Huxley and Frank Arthur, with Huxley reversing the 1929 result by beating Arthur into second place. Huxley received the winners' cheque for £100 plus the Star trophy, while Arthur received £50.

Wembley's last league match was due to take place on 25 September at Coventry but, before it could, the ACU shut down Coventry due to irregularities in connection with the payment of moneys due to their riders. Both the managing director and the secretary of Motordomes Ltd, the company that owned Coventry Speedway, were suspended. Wembley were awarded the match 36-0.

Even without this walkover, Wembley had already clinched the Southern League title, losing only 3 matches all season, winning 19 (20 including the Coventry match) and drawing 1. In a bit of a surprise finish, Southampton managed to pip Stamford Bridge to take the runner-up spot.

The fifth and final Test match of that first Ashes season was held at the Empire Stadium on 26 September. Unfortunately it rained heavily during the day and on into the evening, a fact that upset both the crowd figures and the racing itself as the track was very slippery and cut up quickly. Two Wembley Lions made the England team: Colin Watson, who captained England for the night, and Jack Ormston. Others to ride for England were Gus Kuhn, Frank Varey, Jack Parker, Squib Burton, Frank Charles and Arthur Jervis, with Roger Frogley and Syd Jackson as standby reserves. Australia were represented by Jack Chapman, who had taken Frank Arthur's place due to the latter's illness, Dicky Case, Vic Huxley, Bluey Wilkinson, Billy Lamont, Max Grosskreutz, Charlie Spinks, Ron Johnson and Arnie Hansen.

In spite of a couple of engine failures, England managed to win by four points, 49-45. The two home-track men, Watson and Ormston, were England's top scorers with 8 points each. For Australia Huxley, with 12 points, and Lamont with 10 put up a brave fight but it was not quite enough. The result of this Test meant that England had won the first Ashes series by four matches to one.

In the meantime, the Lions had come through to the final of the *Evening News* London Cup by beating Wimbledon 108-83 on aggregate in the semi-final. The first leg of the final took place on 9 October when Wembley took on their old rivals, Stamford Bridge, at the Empire Stadium. Once again a crowd in excess of 40,000 witnessed the match. Thanks in part to a return to form by Buster Frogley, the Lions took a convincing lead of 22 points (59-37) back to Stamford Bridge for the return leg.

The second and deciding leg took place on 11 October, when around 35,000 spectators crammed into Stamford Bridge to see a thrilling match. After just two heats, the Lions were down by six points but, thanks to some superb riding by George Greenwood and Jack Ormston and some even more brilliant riding by skipper Colin Watson, Wembley pulled the points back, in the end losing the leg by just three points, 49-46, thus taking the first London Cup by 105 points to 86. After the match, Mr Olive, assistant editor of the *Evening News*, presented the cup and gold medals to the victorious Wembley Lions team.

Yet again a crowd of 40,000 turned out on 16 October for the Wembley Gold Cup. Ormston came unstuck in the final while leading Walter Hull, leaving the latter in first place. However, the race was not over and, from a seemingly impossible position, Stamford Bridge captain Gus Kuhn gradually fought his way back in to the race, finally overtaking Hull on the last bend to win the race and the trophy by just a bike's length.

Wembley's official victory meeting was held on 30 October when the team were presented with the *News of the World* Trophy, cheques and medals as winners of the Southern League. The following evening many thousands of Wembley fans packed in to the Empire Stadium for the victory ball.

In a special end-of season challenge, Wembley took on Northern League champions Belle Vue to determine which team had the right to the title British National Champions. In winning the Northern League, Belle Vue had lost just one match all season, but Wembley showed them who was boss by winning both legs and taking the title by 56 points to 43.

Wembley finally closed their season on 13 November with a series of individual events, with Tiger Sanderson winning the junior event and Gus Kuhn the Visitors' Scratch race and the Farewell Handicap. As a finale, the six-year-old mascot Ian Hoskins had a go at the junior record held by Edinburgh's Walter Brierley. Hoskins' time of 86.8 seconds carved no less than fifteen seconds off Brierley's record.

So ended Wembley's second season, a very successful one in which they won the Southern League, the British Championship and the London Cup, while their individual riders had also had a great deal of success, with Ormston winning the London Riders' Championship, Whitfield the Scottish Championship and Watson the Empire Championship (an individual trophy for team captains).

Could Wembley maintain their supremacy in 1931?

1930 League Averages – qualification 6 matches

	Matches	Rides	Points	CMA
Jack Ormston	23	69	173.5	10.06
Colin Watson	18	53	127	9.58
Stan Catlett	10	30	56	7.47
Harry Whitfield	22	66	110.5	6.67
Arthur Atkinson	23	69	113	6.55
George Greenwood	13	37	52	5.62
Buster Frogley	18	54	65	4.81

Southern League Results

Date	H/A	Against	W/L/D	Score
8 May	Home	Leicester	Won	34-20
15 May	Away	Nottingham	Won	31-22

29 May	Away	Leicester	Won	29-25
4 June	Away	Stamford Bridge	Lost	24-29
12 June	Home	Crystal Palace	Won	31-22
19 June	Home	Harringay	Won	33-20
21 June	Away	High Beech	Won	32-21
26 June	Home	Hall Green	Won	28.5-24.5
3 July	Home	Wimbledon	Won	30-22
8 July	Away	West Ham	Won	31-22
10 July	Home	Southampton	Won	35-19
11 July	Away	Harringay	Won	31-23
17 July	Home	Lea Bridge	Won	40-14
19 July	Away	Crystal Palace	Lost	23-30
25 July	Away	Hall Green	Won	35-19
28 July	Away	Wimbledon	Won	32-21
13 August	Away	Lea Bridge	Won	31-23
14 August	Home	High Beech	Won	37-16
20 August	Away	Southampton	Drew	26.5-26.5
28 August	Home	Coventry	Won	39-14
4 September	Home	Stamford Bridge	Lost	24-29
11 September	Home	West Ham	Won	36-18
18 September	Home	Nottingham	Won	37-17
25 September	Away	Coventry	Won	36-0

(The final match against Coventry was awarded as Coventry had had their licence suspended by the ACU.)

London Cup

First Round
Wembley 71 High Beech 25
High Beech 52 Wembley 44
Aggregate: Wembley 115 High Beech 77

Semi-Final
Wembley 52 Wimbledon 44
Wimbledon 39 Wembley 56
Aggregate: Wembley 108 Wimbledon 83

Final
Wembley 59 Stamford Bridge 37
Stamford Bridge 49 Wembley 46
Aggregate: Wembley 105 Stamford Bridge 86

Final League Table

	Played	Won	Drawn	Lost	For	Against	Points
WEMBLEY	24	20	1	3	768	496	41
Southampton	24	17	1	6	716	560	35
Stamford Bridge	24	16	1	7	728.5	551.5	33
Wimbledon	24	16	1	7	695	578	33
Hall Green	24	13	1	10	647	632	27
Coventry	24	13	1	10	629	634	27
Crystal Palace	24	11	1	12	667	613	23
Lea Bridge	24	10	1	13	602.5	672.5	21
West Ham	24	10	0	14	627	647	20
Leicester	24	8	1	15	586.5	689.5	17
High Beech	24	8	0	16	555	720	16
Harringay	24	7	0	17	572.5	707.5	14
Nottingham	24	2	1	21	489	782	5

FOUR

1931 – CONSOLIDATION

By the first dance of the New Year of 1931, the supporters' club had grown to a staggering 24,597. The club itself received a great boost when they were filmed by the Gaumont Company during one of their outings. The film ended with the by-now-famous war cry 'W-E-M-B-L-E-Y' and was shown at all Gaumont and other leading cinemas around the country. Another outing undertaken by the club before the season started was to Buster Frogley's farm in Hoddesdon, Hertfordshire, where Frogley showed off his new aeroplane plus some new JAP bikes that were under test ready for the new season.

Eleven teams began the 1931 Southern League season, Coventry and Hall Green having dropped out. This year each team would ride against each other four times, twice at home and twice away. The draw for the London Cup took place in February with Wembley being drawn against Wimbledon in the first round. The Empire Stadium was selected as the venue for the third Test in August.

Because of the success of the team in 1930, Hoskins was inundated with applications from riders wishing to ride for the Lions. He retained the services of Watson as captain, Ormston, Frogley, Whitfield, Catlett, Jackson, Evans and Greenwood. The latter two had spent a very successful close season riding in New Zealand, where Greenwood had broken the track record at Christchurch. Among those leaving were Sanderson, who joined West Ham, Sticpewich, who went to Rochdale, and Fairweather, who headed for Nottingham. Atkinson was unfit following a late injury the previous season and his future remained uncertain. Just before the season started, Hoskins received a cable from Catlett, saying that he would not be returning to England. This was a big blow for Wembley as the Aussie star looked to have a great future in the sport.

At the beginning of 1931 West Ham announced they were in financial difficulties and might be forced to close. The Wembley management decided to step in and took over the running of speedway at Custom House. To give them the best possible start to the season, therefore, it was agreed that their opening fixture would be a challenge match against the mighty Lions. The match took place on a bitterly cold evening, 31 March, in front of the guests of honour, the Mayor and Mayoress of West Ham, and 30,000 spectators. Wembley came out on top by 28 points to 24. Watson was the star of the night, ably supported by Jackson and Frogley.

Because they were now under the same management, Sir Arthur Elvin took the decision to run coaches to West Ham from Wembley on race nights. At the Hammers' second meeting, on 3 April, eleven coaches left the Empire Stadium to a meeting affected by an incessant downpour of rain. It took nearly one hour to run four races and the final straw came when the tractor refused to start and officials abandoned the event.

Watson continued the good form he had shown at West Ham by setting up a new record of 19 seconds (48.33mph) in the British Quarter-Mile Championship at Crystal Palace. He also broke the one-lap record at West Ham and then won the £100 Championship at Wimbledon, all in the space of ten days.

Because of his early season form and the fact that he had won the Empire Championship at the tail end of 1930, Watson was chosen as one of the first two riders to compete for a prestigious new competition that was introduced in 1931, the British Match Race Championship. His opponent was the great Vic Huxley. The idea of the competition was that two riders would race a series of match races for the title; the best of three at each rider's home track and, if it was a tie after that, a further best-of-three decider at a neutral track. Reigning Star Champion Huxley was named as the first champion with Watson as his first challenger. The Speedway Control Board would then nominate further challengers (later regularised to a monthly basis) to challenge for the title. Watson surprised many pundits by taking a leg off Huxley and forcing the series to a decider, even though, in the end, he lost 2-1.

Back at Wembley, Elvin had decided to make a night out at the Empire Stadium the cheapest speedway in the country by reducing the price for supporters' club members from 7d to 6d. The Empire Stadium opened its doors for the season on 7 May with a match against old favourites Stamford Bridge. It looked as though Elvin's gamble of reducing prices had paid off handsomely as a record crowd of over 60,000 attended the meeting on a glorious sunny evening.

The Lions were on top form, although Arthur Warwick finished the evening unbeaten for the Pensioners. But it was a victory for Wembley by 31 points to 22. Their second home match, on 14 May, was to prove even more decisive as they hammered Crystal Palace 41-12. During this match, Ormston was fined 10s by the steward for 'jumping at the start'. Nevertheless, he won three races, with Watson and Whitfield winning two each.

The Lions' next match was away at Wimbledon. Frogley was dropped to make way for Jackson. Brilliant team riding by Watson and Evans gave the Lions a great start in heat one, but the Dons hit back immediately with Dicky Case and Ernie Evans in heat two to level the scores. By heat six, Wembley had edged ahead and they managed to maintain their lead, taking the match by 30 points to 22.

Three days later, back at the Lions' den, Wembley entertained their sister track, West Ham. This match saw probably the best race of the season as Ormston and the Hammers' ace Tiger Stevenson battled it out neck and neck for four laps before Ormston just got the verdict by half a wheel on the line. The crowd let out a tremendous cheer that, it was said, was heard in Harrow, some five miles away. Not to be outdone, Watson then set the fastest time of the season, 79.6 seconds. The Lions raced on to win the match 32-22.

In mid-May, Hoskins pulled off another shrewd signing, a new Aussie sensation by the name of Lionel Van Praag. Hoskins told the crowd, 'He [Van Praag] is going to take a few weeks to settle down on the small English circuits but will soon find his true form.' While he was still 'finding his true form', Van Praag was put into the Cubs team. Hoskins had heard about Van Praag from Frank Arthur, even though, in fact, Arthur worked for Wembley's great rivals, International Speedways Ltd (ISL), who he had also told about about Van Praag. He enthused: 'He is the one outstanding rider left in Australia.' Arthur warned the ISL board that Van Praag

The young Lionel Van Praag in action.

was as shrewd a businessman as he was good a rider and that his signature would not be easy to get. To make sure they got his signature, Arthur, together with a representative from ISL, went to Southampton to meet Van Praag as he got off the boat but, when they arrived, he was nowhere to be seen. After some enquiries they learnt that he had got off at a French port and travelled overland. They later discovered they had been outwitted by Hoskins, who had got in first and signed him up for Wembley while he was still en route.

The date 27 May saw the Lions at Lea Bridge. Being away made no difference to the supremely confident Lions as they slaughtered them 36-18, winning every heat. Ormston was unbeaten while Watson and Greenwood both won two races. Lea Bridge had their revenge in the supporting match as their Colts beat the Cubs by 13 points to 8.

Three days later Wembley were away to Stamford Bridge and it was felt that, at last, their unbeaten run might come to an end. The Pensioners supporters, however, very quickly fell silent as, after just two heats, the Lions were already 8 points up, having gained 5-1s in both. Stamford Bridge captain Gus Kuhn tried to lead a fightback but it was too late and the Lions emerged victorious yet again, this time by 30 points to 23. Van Praag made his first appearance in Lions' colours in the second half. He showed his potential by winning the scratch race final.

At about this time, Jack Ormston came up with a novel way of signing autographs for his adoring fans. He had a rubber stamp made and would stamp it on the ladies' arms and legs.

With the Lions now so successful, large crowds turned up every week at the Empire Stadium, many arriving as early as 6.30 p.m. Elvin knew that these crowds needed to be entertained before the match started and so he organised various acts to play, including massed bands, trick cyclists and motorbike stunt riders.

Both Watson and Ormston were selected for the first Test at Crystal Palace. A huge contingent of Wembley supporters made their way to the Sydenham track to cheer on their favourites and the rest of the England team. Unfortunately for the Lions' fans, Watson did not have a good night, being let down by his machinery as three times he was in the lead only for his motor to pack up.

A number of changes took place in the league make-up as first Leicester withdrew to be replaced by Coventry and then, in a big shock to the speedway world, Harringay announced it was to close. Two days after that, Hall Green returned to the fold to take Harringay's place under the name of Birmingham. But, just three days later, they decided they couldn't return after all. The leading London promoters, including Elvin, then approached the Northern League champions Belle Vue to ask if they were prepared to enter a team in the Southern League to replace Harringay. With their ready acceptance and agreement to race under the name Manchester, so as not to cause any confusion, the Southern League was back to eleven teams.

Another new trophy had been introduced this year, the National Trophy, aimed at bringing together the Southern and Northern Leagues in a two-leg knock-out cup tournament. The Lions' first match was against West Ham. With the Hammers losing on their own track by 8 points in the first leg, the second leg back at the Empire Stadium looked a foregone conclusion. Even so, 51,000 spectators were present to see the Lions duly whip West Ham by 56 points to 37 to give an aggregate score of 108-81.

Following a league match at Lea Bridge on 27 June, the emergency committee of the ACU met to consider the cases of Harry Whitfield and George Greenwood. It was alleged that these two had been guilty of conduct prejudicial to the sport inasmuch as they had put up an unsatisfactory performance during one of the races. The substance of the complaint was that the ACU steward at Lea Bridge had accused them of slowing down the final race to enable Harry Whitfield to win it. The emergency committee upheld the allegation and suspended both riders for one month. Elvin and Hoskins were alarmed by this decision and had visions of the league title slipping from their grasp as two of their leading riders missed a number of vital matches. Elvin quickly slapped in an appeal and told the two riders to dress smartly and to look and act like perfect gentlemen before the appeal panel, the Track Control Committee. After hearing the two riders' version of events, the committee found in favour of the ACU steward but felt that the one month's suspension was too harsh and reduced it to seven days.

For the next home meeting, on 2 July, Wembley called up Wally Kilmister and Col Stewart from the Cubs to replace the two suspended riders. With the team pulling together they managed to dispose of the previous year's runners-up, Southampton, by 31 points to 23.

The first leg of the first round of the London Cup was held on 6 July at Wimbledon. Whitfield and Greenwood were now back in the team but, unfortunately, Watson was injured and unable to take part. The Dons, meanwhile, had strengthened their team by signing up the great Vic Huxley from the now-defunct Harringay team. But there was minor tragedy in store for Wimbledon as, in his first ride, Huxley hit a bump on the track, came off, sustained concussion and was unable to take part in the rest of the meeting. It was a close-run affair after that but, with Whitfield just getting the better of Case in his last ride and the Dons' captain Kempster suffering machine trouble, the Lions just scraped home by four points, 50-46.

The return leg took place on 9 July, when once again the Dons were at full strength while the Lions were still without their captain. Wembley had a great start as Ormston led heat one from start to finish while his partner, Frogley, brought the house down, pipping Kempster by half a wheel, giving the Lions a flying 5-1 start. However, Wimbledon fought back and by the interval had established a three-point lead, leaving them one behind on aggregate. In the first race after the interval, the 40,000 fans were on their toes as Ormston and Frogley beat Huxley into third place. This was followed by another 5-1 to the Lions as Evans and Shelton took first

Wally Kilmister.

and second places in the next heat. A see-saw battle took place as the Dons took a 5-1 in the following heat, heat twelve, and Whitfield and Kilmister managed a 5-0 in heat thirteen thanks to Kempster falling and Claude Rye breaking a chain.

With just one heat to go, Wembley led by four points. Huxley took the lead from the start with Greenwood close behind him. After two laps, Greenwood managed to pass Huxley with one of the best moves seen all season. He held on to win the race and gain a 3-3 for the Lions, who won the match by 49 points to 45, giving them an overall victory of 99-91.

Just a few hours before this match took place, Wembley had installed a new set of speakers, said to be the finest in the country.

On 11 July the Lions rode at Sheffield in the second round of the National Trophy and took the home side apart. Only Dusty Haigh and Gus Platts put up any sort of show for Sheffield and Wembley ran out winners 55-41.

The Lions next match was at Sydenham, away to Crystal Palace. Given the relative strengths of the two teams, it was felt that the points were in the bag for Wembley but the Crystal Palace team were all mounted on their new Wallis JAP machines. As it turned out, the Lions won just two heats all night thanks to Ormston and Greenwood, while the Glaziers' captain, Ron Johnson, was unbeaten and registered the fastest time of the evening. The final score was Crystal Palace 30 Wembley 23. This was only the third time the Lions had been beaten in a league match this season. Fourteen coachloads of Wembley fans had made their way to south London but they returned disappointed.

The National Trophy return leg against Sheffield took place on 23 July and saw Wembley almost whitewash Sheffield, winning by 70 points to 25, 125-66 on aggregate. Nine heats were won by a maximum 5-1. Watson made his welcome return for this match, winning three heats, while Ormston and Whitfield went one better, winning four each.

There was a further problem for the league as, on 25 July, Nottingham withdrew. This time no team took their place. This now left ten teams in the Southern League. Meanwhile the Northern League had suffered even more withdrawals and was left with just six teams running. It seemed inevitable that for 1932 a new National League would have to be introduced. Some promoters were against the idea as it would lead to increased costs and travelling expenses. The idea was shelved until the winter.

Ormston was well-known outside speedway circles as an aviator and in July 1931 he put up one of the best performances of his career when he took part in the King's Cup Air Race, flying his Westland Widgeon monoplane. He averaged 93mph and finished seventeenth out of forty-one starters. He was so pleased with his plane's performance that when he later got a cat he named it Widgeon.

Crystal Palace, the team that had shocked Wembley twelve days earlier, visited the Empire Stadium on 31 July for a league fixture. Mounted on their Wallis JAPs again, they were expected to do well and, after three heats, they seemed to be living up to that expectation as they were just three points behind. However, after this good start, they faded and the Lions pushed ahead, finally winning the match by 34 points to 19. Watson won all his races and was the only rider to beat Johnson.

But Wembley were still not having things their own way as they followed the Crystal Palace match with a visit to Coventry. In another minor surprise, Coventry defeated the Lions. Hoskins was concerned that one or two members were not pulling their weight and he threatened drastic changes if things didn't improve.

Perhaps the surprise of the season happened on 5 August when Lions' reserve Colin Stewart defeated Buster Frogley in a time of 79.6 seconds to win Wembley's eliminating round of the Star Championship, thereby qualifying for the final.

After the shock of his elimination, Frogley rode a blinder in the subsequent league match against Coventry, winning all his races and helping his team to a 37-17 victory and some revenge for the loss to the same team earlier in the week.

The Lions made their first league visit to Manchester on 19 August. In spite of a sodden track, Wembley put up a terrific show, winning eight heats out of the nine, though they lost 28-26. Greenwood won three races. Unfortunately it was a bad-tempered match. The most serious incident occurred in the pits when one of the Wembley riders lost his temper and struck a pits marshal.

The following evening, after a hectic journey home, Wembley rode a double-header at the Empire Stadium. First up was a match against Wimbledon who, although they were without Billy Lamont and Dicky Case, managed to hold the Lions to a 27-27 draw, with Huxley winning three races.

The second match was against the High Beech Foresters. Solid riding by Phil Bishop and Tiger Hart kept the visitors in the match for the first half but gradually the Lions managed to pull themselves together and ran out victors by 31 points to 23.

The third Test was due to be held at Wembley on 14 August but, owing to high winds and rain, it was postponed until the following week, 21 August. By 6.30 p.m. over 10,000 cars were already parked in the stadium car park. In the end a crowd of 60,000 were admitted.

Preston star H.R. 'Ginger' Lees proved to be the surprise packege of the night. Having never seen the Wembley track before, let alone ridden it, he won his first race in a time just three-fifths of a second outside the track record. Two Wembley riders took part for England, Watson, who scored three, and Whitfield, who scored two. Stewart rode for Australia, scoring three.

The following week, Wembley returned to their best form, beating Southampton by 32 points to 22. The second half saw a welcome return to the saddle by Arthur Atkinson.

On 29 August the Lions travelled to Stamford Bridge for the first leg of the London Cup semi-final. There was always something about the matches between these two London rivals that appealed to all speedway fans and once again a record crowd gathered to witness the encounter. There was a lot of tension out on the track as well as a lot of needle and both the Pensioners' Frank Arthur and Wembley's George Greenwood were warned twice for starting offences.

One of the strangest races of the season happened in heat fourteen of this match, when Colin Watson developed engine trouble on the second lap. With Wembley's other rider already out of the race, Watson ambled round hoping to keep going long enough for third place, only to find both Bridge riders, Dicky Smythe and Fred Ralph, piled up in the safety fence. Watson therefore won the race in a time of 110.8 seconds. Ralph pushed home for second place, collapsing on the line. Van Praag took part in this match for the Lions, only to fall heavily and sustain facial injuries requiring six stitches. The final score was Stamford Bridge 50 Wembley 44, leaving all to race for in the second leg.

This took place on 3 September. The spectators, who again numbered close on 60,000, saw one of the best meetings of the season, a real ding-dong battle. For three heats the scoring was level. Then the Lions scored a 4-2, leaving themselves four points behind overall. Gradually Wembley pulled back the deficit. With one heat to go, the score on the night was 49.5-39.5, making the aggregate scores Wembley 93.5 Stamford Bridge 89.5. If Stamford Bridge could manage a 5-1 in the last heat they could still draw level overall.

As they shot away from the start it was the Stamford Bridge pair, Gus Kuhn and Bill Stanley, who took the lead. It seemed as though the Pensioners would get their much-needed 5-1. Jumping up and down at the pit gate, Hoskins showed unmistakable symptoms of bursting a blood vessel. But he was saved as Kuhn came unstuck on the top bend and slid to the ground. This seemed to upset Stanley, who slowed, allowing Ormston to pass him to give Wembley a 4-2 and the match. Hoskins' hat went up in the air, followed by Hoskins himself, who celebrated with a flying drop kick on his headgear. He was joined by the riders and officials as they all gave vent to their pent-up feelings. Hoskins' hat was ruined but he didn't care. His team were through to the final by 98.5 to 90.5.

The Lions paid another visit to Manchester on 9 September. This time they put their first-meeting defeat well and truly behind them as, riding magnificently, they thumped the Aces, winning by a margin of 20 points. Star performer for Wembley was Greenwood, solidly backed by Kilmister, Ormston, Van Praag and Whitfield.

However, tragedy struck at the meeting as, in heat two, home rider Indian Allen fell and was rushed to hospital suffering from skull and rib injuries. He died in hospital the following Saturday.

Speedway's big night of the year, the Star Championship Trophy, was once again held at the Empire Stadium on 18 September. Each track sent two representatives who had come through

The 1931 Wembley team that did so well that they made the front cover of the 10 October edition of the *Speedway News*.

the qualifying rounds on their own track. The pre-meeting favourite was Jack Parker, with Vic Huxley, Ron Johnson and Frank Arthur just behind, but there was a surprise winner in Wimbledon's American ace Ray Tauser.

Parker qualified for the final but was badly trapped on the first bend and crossed the inner white line, for which he was disqualified. Tauser then battled it out for four laps with his Wimbledon teammate Huxley before proving victorious on the line. West Ham's Tommy Croombs was third. Wembley's two representatives, Watson and Stewart, were a little disappointing and never really showed.

The following evening Wembley were at Crystal Palace for the first leg of the *Evening News* London Cup final. The Lions were without two of their leading riders, Greenwood and Whitfield, who were replaced by Shelton and Frogley. Frogley had recently been dropped from the team to make way for the ever-improving Norman Evans.

Once again the Glaziers got the better of the Lions on their own track, winning by the wide margin of 23 points, 59-36. The return at the Empire Stadium looked like being a cracker, with Wembley having to make up such a large deficit, but the team put on a rather lacklustre performance. Not only did they not make up the 23 points but, for the first time in their history, they actually lost a home cup tie.

Crystal Palace, mounted on their Wallis machines, took a strong lead right from the start and by heat seven were already 10 points up and never looked to be in any danger of losing. The final score on the night was Wembley 40 Crystal Palace 55, making the final aggregate score 114-76 to the Glaziers, who thus became London Cup champions for 1931.

The Lions made up for their poor performance the following week when they tore through the Stamford Bridge team 34-19 and then, in the second match of a double-header, did slightly better against Lea Bridge, winning 34-18. These two victories ensured that, although they had lost the London Cup, the Southern League title was theirs for the second year running.

Greenwood and Whitfield returned for the National Trophy final first leg, held on 8 October at the Empire Stadium. This time there was no mistake in a cup final for the Lions as they rode like real champions, pulling the Bridge team apart. Only Frank Arthur put up any sort of opposition and Wembley won the match with ease, 71-24. Van Praag scored a maximum 12 points, while the rest of the team gave strong support, Greenwood scoring 11, Watson, Whitfield and Kilmister 9 each, Ormston 8, Evans 7 and Jackson 6.

In the return leg two days later, the Pensioners put up a much better display despite being without Dicky Case (injured at Wembley), Gus Kuhn and Wal Phillips, but it was still a victory for Wembley by 49 points to 45.

Unfortunately, the Lions suffered two serious injuries during the match as, in heat twelve, Greenwood fell and Jackson, his partner, ran into him. A medical examination revealed that Greenwood had fractured his shoulder while Jackson had broken his collarbone.

After the meeting, the Lions were presented with the *Daily Mail* National Trophy and medals by the speedway journalist Mr Tom Webster.

The following table sets out the Wembley riders' performance in National Trophy matches for 1931:

Rider	Matches	Rides	1st	2nd	3rd	Points Scored	CMA
Colin Watson	7	28	15	9	4	67	9.57
Jack Ormston	8	32	13	14	4	71	8.86
George Greenwood	8	29	13	11	2	63	8.69
Harry Whitfield	6	22	9	6	4	43	7.82
Lionel Van Praag	8	32	12	10	6	62	7.75
Norman Evans	8	32	10	11	6	58	7.25
Buster Frogley	3	12	1	6	3	18	6.00
Wally Kilmister	7	28	4	7	11	37	5.29
Colin Stewart	3	7	1	2	2	9	5.14
Charlie Shelton	4	11	1	1	4	9	3.27
Jack Jackson	5	19	0	2	11	15	3.16

The final Southern League match against Coventry, due to be held on 29 October, was abandoned and instead a combined Wembley and West Ham team rode a challenge match against 'The Rest'. At this meeting, Wembley were presented with their Southern League trophy and medals.

The last meeting of the season took place on 5 November and was a Best Pairs competition, won by Jack Parker and Bluey Wilkinson.

With another successful season behind them, in which they had won the Southern League and National Trophy double, a number of the Lions set sail for the Antipodes; Van Praag for Sydney, Kilmister for Wellington, Stewart for Victoria and Jackson to New Zealand.

1931 League Averages – qualification 6 matches

	Matches	Rides	Points	CMA
Colin Watson	34	102	226.5	8.88
Jack Ormston	34	100	207	8.28
George Greenwood	31	90	175	7.78
Lionel Van Praag	21	55	92	6.69
Harry Whitfield	32	92	150	6.52
Norman Evans	30	90	133	5.91
Wally Kilmister	17	42	61	5.81
Buster Frogley	15	45	61	5.42
Jack Jackson	10	24	26	4.33

Southern League matches

Date	H/A	Against	W/L/D	Score
23 April	Away	Leicester	Won	31-22
30 April	Away	Nottingham	Won	28-26
2 May	Away	High Beech	Lost	24-30
7 May	Home	Stamford Bridge	Won	31-22
14 May	Home	Crystal Palace	Won	41-12
18 May	Away	Wimbledon	Won	30-22
21 May	Home	West Ham	Won	32-22
27 May	Away	Lea Bridge	Won	36-18
30 May	Away	Stamford Bridge	Won	30-23
4 June	Home	Wimbledon	Won	31-22
18 June	Home	High Beech	Won	43-11
18 June	Home	Nottingham	Won	37-16
20 June	Away	Crystal Palace	Won	36-16
23 June	Away	West Ham	Won	29-24
25 June	Home	Manchester	Won	37-16
2 July	Home	Southampton	Won	31-23
4 July	Away	Southampton	Lost	23-31
16 July	Home	Lea Bridge	Won	34-20
18 July	Away	Crystal Palace	Lost	23-30
30 July	Home	Crystal Palace	Won	34-19
4 August	Away	Coventry	Lost	25-29
6 August	Home	Coventry	Won	37-17
15 August	Away	High Beech	Won	33-20
19 August	Away	Manchester	Lost	26-28
20 August	Home	Wimbledon	Drew	27-27
20 August	Home	High Beech	Won	31-23
27 August	Home	Southampton	Won	32-22
9 September	Away	Manchester	Won	36-16

10 September	Home	West Ham	Won	29.5-24.5
10 September	Home	Manchester	Won	30-22
14 September	Away	Wimbledon	Lost	25-28
19 September	Away	Lea Bridge	Won	32-22
22 September	Away	West Ham	Won	32-20
1 October	Home	Stamford Bridge	Won	34-19
1 October	Home	Lea Bridge	Won	34-18
3 October	Away	Southampton	Lost	24-30
17 October	Away	Stamford Bridge	Lost	21-32
29 October	Home	Coventry	Abandoned	–

Final League Table

	Played	Won	Drawn	Lost	For	Against	Points
WEMBLEY	38	29	1	8	1,149.5	822.5	59
Stamford Bridge	38	27	0	11	1,117.5	890.5	54
West Ham	38	23	0	15	1,065	944	46
Crystal Palace	38	22	0	16	1,040	964	44
Wimbledon	38	19	1	18	1,014.5	995.5	39
High Beech	38	19	1	18	950	1,036	39
Southampton	38	18	0	20	1,027	990	36
Manchester	38	14	0	24	916	1,091	28
Lea Bridge	38	11	0	27	906	1,115	22
Coventry	38	8	1	29	825	1,091	17
Nottingham	19	8	0	11	467.5	538.5	16

(Nottingham withdrew during the season but their records were retained)

National Trophy

First Round
Wembley: Bye

Second Round
Wembley 56 West Ham 37
West Ham 44 Wembley 52
Aggregate: Wembley 108 West Ham 81

Third Round
Wembley 70 Sheffield 25
Sheffield 41 Wembley 55
Aggregate: Wembley 125 Sheffield 66

Semi-Final
Wembley 48 Wimbledon 47

Wimbledon 46 Wembley 49
Aggregate: Wembley 97 Wimbledon 93

Final
Wembley 71 Stamford Bridge 24
Stamford Bridge 45 Wembley 49
Aggregate: Wembley 120 Stamford Bridge 69

London Cup

First Round
Wembley 49 Wimbledon 45
Wimbledon 46 Wembley 50
Aggregate: Wembley 99 Wimbledon 91

Semi-Final
Wembley 53.5 Stamford Bridge 41.5
Stamford Bridge 50 Wembley 44
Aggregate: Wembley 97.5 Stamford Bridge 91.5

Final
Crystal Palace 59 Wembley 36
Wembley 40 Crystal Palace 55
Aggregate: Crystal Palace 114 Wembley 76

NO. 2 – WALLY KILMISTER

Kilmister was the first New Zealander to make a real impact on British speedway. He was born in Karori, Wellington in 1907. At the age of fourteen he was apprenticed to a firm of motor engineers. He soon bought his own motorcycle and made his track debut at the age of seventeen on the grass track at Otaki, some fifty miles from Wellington. He was so successful that he was quickly given a works contract by the New Zealand agent for AJS motorcycles. After winning the New Zealand Grass Track Championship he was prevailed upon by his sponsor to take a look at the new sport of dirt track racing, which was being tried out at Kilbirnie Stadium in Wellington. He attended a few practice sessions but quickly came to the conclusion that he had very little aptitude for this new form of racing and decided to go back to the grass track. A few days before the first proper meeting was due to take place at Kilbirnie on 9 March 1929, two Australians, Gus Clifton and Max Graham, arrived and persuaded Kilmister to try his luck on a Douglas. Mounted on his new machine, he flew round the track, proving to be easily the best of the local lads. His only loss came in the Golden Helmet final, when he was beaten by the far more experienced Graham.

It was during the 1929/30 season that he rose to stardom on New Zealand tracks and initially held both the Four-Lap Rolling Start and Four-Lap Flying Start records at Kilbirnie as well as taking the Golden Helmet title. Although he lost both the track records to Lionel Van Praag at one meeting in late 1929, he managed to successfully defend his Golden Helmet title against Van Praag and another top Australian star, Charlie Spinks, at the same meeting.

By the end of the season he had made such a name for himself as the uncrowned king of New Zealand speedway that he was advised to travel to England. Kilmister himself was sceptical and thought that the standard would be far too high for him in England. Undeterred, the manager at the Kilbirnie track cabled Johnnie Hoskins who, to Kilmister's complete astonishment, cabled back offering not only a contract to ride for Wembley but also to pay his fare over.

After starting off in Wembley's junior team, the Cubs, in 1930, Kilmister made the full Lions team occasionally but was not able to rise above reserve in his first two seasons. It was in the second half of the 1932 season that it all suddenly seemed to click with him, and he quickly rose to become one of the team's leading riders, topping the Lions' averages the following year, 1933, with a cma of 9.33, scoring eight full maximums during the season. He remained a heat leader with the Lions until 1935 but in 1936 he suffered from a number of injuries that badly

Wally Kilmister.

affected his form and at one point he even dropped down to reserve. He never really recovered from the injuries and, at the end of the 1938 season, Wally announced his intention to spend more time with his business, a sports goods shop in Wembley.

During 1939 he decided he would like to have another go but, with his new crop of youngsters, Alec Jackson found he had no room for him in the Wembley team and loaned him out to Southampton instead. Wally was unable to recapture his form of the early 1930s, scoring just five points from four matches.

He did not return to racing after the Second World War, though he did become an influential figure in New Zealand speedway circles. One of his protégées, Bruce Abernethy, went on to become a Wembley rider himself.

He never made the World Championship final but did make one appearance in the Star Riders' final in 1935. Unfortunately he fell in his first ride and took no further part in the meeting.

Being a New Zealander he did not have much opportunity to represent his country at international level, but he was selected to ride for a Dominions team against England in 1938, scoring 13 points in two matches. He also rode in a number of unofficial Test matches in his native New Zealand, including three matches against England in the 1930/31 season and one against the USA in the 1935/36 season. He also won the New Zealand Championship in 1936.

As an all-round motorcyclist he accomplished a number of other feats. He was awarded the Brooklands Gold Star for lapping the course at over 100mph and, at one time, held the New Zealand one-mile land-speed record of 107mph.

Like a number of his Wembley teammates, he was also an accomplished pilot.

FIVE

1932 – THE TREBLE

As expected, 1932 saw the amalgamation of the Southern and Northern Leagues into one National League, with the following ten teams taking part: Belle Vue, Coventry, Crystal Palace, Plymouth, Sheffield, Southampton, Stamford Bridge, Wembley, West Ham and Wimbledon. The season was to be divided into two halves, with each team meeting once home and away in the first half for the National Speedway Association Cup and in the second half for the National League itself. The National Trophy and London Cup were to continue as before and there was also to be a London Reserve League, with four riders per side competing over four heats.

Sir Arthur Elvin, never frightened to open his chequebook, signed a further three riders for the new season, Reg Bounds from West Ham, Preston's Ginger Lees and Gordon Byers from Leeds. He also welcomed back former Lion, Australian Stan Catlett. Along with the four new signings, Wembley retained Watson, Ormston, Greenwood, Van Praag, Evans, Kilmister, Stewart, Jackson and Shelton from the 1931 line-up. Those leaving were Buster Frogley, who had decided to retire, and Arthur Atkinson, who made the short trip across to Wembley's sister track West Ham.

A grand reopening dance was held at the Empire Stadium on 14 April, with over 2,500 people packing the floor to meet their favourite riders. In fact, the Lions had already made their first track appearance at Wimbledon in a challenge match on 11 April. With Watson ruled out of the match through an injury sustained at West Ham's opening meeting, newcomers Bounds and Lees were drafted into the team to ride as a pair and rode exceptionally well, though the outstanding pair was, not for the first time, Greenford and Whitfield. Their team riding was superb. In fact, it has been said that they invented the art of team riding as we now know it. Byers also made his debut for the Lions and won two of his races. Acting captain for the evening Jack Ormston was top scorer with 11 points, leading his team to victory by 51 points to 40.

Two days later, Wembley took part in their first league match of the season as they took on Southampton at Bannister Court. Watson was still unavailable but his deputy, Ormston, went one better than his previous performance by scoring a maximum. The Lions took first place in eight out of the nine races, but only managed to win by five points, 29-24.

The following match saw Wembley at Plymouth, this time winning more comfortably, by 36 to 15. Two days later they were due at Coventry but the heavy rain put paid to that.

By the time of Wembley's first home fixture against Stamford Bridge, Elvin was able to announce that the supporters' club was receiving applications at the rate of 1,500 per day. One

Ginger Lees.

of Britain's greatest aviators, the Master of Sempill, was so keen to see the match that he flew 400 miles from Glasgow during the afternoon to be present. But it wasn't a great meeting as the Pensioners rode well below par. Jack Chapman had been forced to withdraw on the orders of the track doctor, Arthur rode in a great deal of pain and Kuhn seemed completely out of sorts. With Watson back for the Lions, the result was a comfortable victory for them as they beat their old rivals 31-21.

Wembley's next match was a much closer affair as they took on Crystal Palace at Sydenham on 30 April. By heat four the Lions were leading by one point, 12-11. The Glaziers, however, clawed their way back and a 5-1 from Nobby Key and Ron Johnson in heat eight, after Johnson had ridden magnificently to pass Lees, saw them now move into a five-point lead with just one race to go. Although this resulted in a 5-1 for Greenwood and Whitfield, it meant that Wembley had suffered their first loss of the season, by just one point, 27-26.

Always looking for new ways to encourage support, Elvin now announced that the club would produce its own supporters' magazine, to be called *Red and White*. Edited by R. Talmage-Morton, the first issue went on sale on 12 May and cost 2d.

On that same day, the Lions travelled up to Belle Vue. Both teams were at full strength and a close match was expected. On their own track, however, Aces' stars Frank Varey and Eric Langton were just too good for the Londoners and both scored maximum points. Greenwood was the pick of the Lions, winning two races, but, in general, the Wembley team were no match for Belle Vue, losing out 29-25.

Back home for their next match, the Lions once again found an opposition rider walking off with maximum points in the person of Wimbledon's Dicky Case. This time, however, the top man did not receive sufficient backing from his team and the Lions were able to take the match 28-24.

With two defeats and just a four-point win at home, Elvin had some strong words for Hoskins, telling him to get the Lions back on top where they belonged, or else! Hoskins passed this message on to his team and it was a hapless Southampton side that felt the full force of the onslaught as Hoskins and his team set out to prove that they were far from finished, decimating the Saints by 37 points to 16. This was followed by a stunning away victory at Sheffield on 25 May, as Wembley ran out winners by 34 points to 20, in spite of Sheffield's top rider, Squib Burton, winning all his races.

At the start of June, Wembley found themselves in the unaccustomed position of second place in the league, as Belle Vue held on to top spot. However, Wembley were only behind on points average and had one match in hand over the Aces.

There was good news for Jack Ormston as he learned that he had passed his air pilot exams and had been granted a full licence, which entitled him to carry passengers. Interestingly, Ormston was not the only pilot among the Wembley line-up. Greenwood, Kilmister and Van Praag all held pilot's certificates, while Catlett was also learning to fly at Buster Frogley's aerodrome at Broxbourne.

On 16 June the Wembley Gold Cup was held. Most of the top riders of the day took part, including Vic Huxley, Jack Parker, Squib Burton, Dicky Case, Bluey Wilkinson, Ron Johnson, Tom Farndon, Tiger Stevenson, Billy Lamont and the French champion Charles Bellisent, as well as the top Wembley riders. After a hard-fought meeting, the four finalists were Ormston, Lees, Stevenson and Johnson. Johnson shot away from the start and won the race by a distance. The Wembley pair, Lees and Ormston, finished second and third respectively.

The second Test match of the season was held at Wembley on 23 June. Three Lions were picked for the England team, Lees, Greenwood and Ormston, while Van Praag was selected by the Australians, though he was dropped just prior to the meeting owing to loss of form. The Aussies were on top form that night; Lamont and Case gave probably the most brilliant display of team riding yet seen in this country, outclassing their opponents in every race they rode and finishing the night unbeaten as a pair, while Huxley and Wilkinson each scored 9 points and Arthur 8. Only Greenwood and Ormston seemed capable of matching the Kangaroos, scoring 8 and 7. The final score was England 35 Australia 59.

The club organised a day's outing on 26 June to a special sports meeting held at Pole Hill Farm, Hillingdon. This was a complete day out with events such as musical chairs on motorcycles, grass track racing, a car relay race and a motorcycle polo match between Wembley and West Ham. This thrilling day of motor sport was captured on film and shown at a number of cinemas.

By the end of June, Watson had inexplicably lost form. Some of it was put down to mechanical failures, but he said he felt tired so he decided to drop himself from the team for a short rest. He handed over the captaincy of the team to Ormston. Whitfield was another not riding to his potential and he dropped down to reserve. Hoskins announced the new team line-up would be Ormston (captain) and Kilmister, promoted from the Cubs; Greenwood and Bounds; Lees and Byers with Van Praag and Whitfield as reserves.

Ginger Lees won one of the season's biggest individual meetings on 4 July when he took on and beat riders of the calibre of Huxley, Farndon, Wilkinson, Lamont, Grosskreutz and Case in the 1932 Wimbledon Open Championship, an event open only to Test match riders. His reward was a £300 cheque.

Tow days later, 6 July saw the full team take part in a crucial match away to Stamford Bridge. Whichever team won would take the National Speedway Association Cup. Unfortunately the Lions put up a miserable performance while the Pensioners just romped away from the start – three of their team, Arthur, Phillips and Warwick, scoring maximums – to win by 37 points to 17. Wembley had no-one with a score higher than 3.

With the end of the National Speedway Association Cup the teams now lined up for the National League itself, with just one team, Sheffield, dropping out and Clapton replacing Southampton. Before the start of the National League, Jack Jackson was transferred to Plymouth.

The new league competition started well for Wembley. Their first match in the National League took place at the Empire Stadium against Clapton on 14 July. The result was a comfortable 33-20 victory.

The following week saw a much closer match against Wimbledon. Although Wembley won by four points the result could have been very different if the Dons' Dicky Case had not blown his engine up and their American star, Ray Tauser, had not had his best machine impounded at the docks by Customs. In the end, however, it was Lees who finally won the match for the Lions. At the end of heat eight, the scores were 25-23 to Wembley, so there was all still to race for. As the riders reached the first bend in the final heat, Lees found himself sandwiched between Wimbledon's celebrated Australian Test pairing, Billy Lamont and Dick Case. A 5-1 to the Dons' pair would give them the match by two points. It seemed impossible that Lees could get through but, ignoring all danger, he laid his bike over at an almost suicidal angle and shot clear. With Case falling on the third lap, the result was a 4-2 for the Lions and a 29-25 winning scoreline.

Away at Plymouth for their next match, the Lions had a much easier time of it. The match was virtually over by heat four, as Wembley went into a 17-6 lead, eventually winning the match 35-16.

The next away match was expected to be much tougher as Coventry had already defeated Stamford Bridge and Belle Vue but, on a rain-soaked track, the experience of the Lions' riders came to the fore. Lees led the charge with 9 points while Whitfield contributed 6. Only Skid Pitcher was able to match them for Coventry, scoring 7 points. The final score was Coventry 22 Wembley 29.

Wembley were now well on course to win the first ever National League title. But they were not prepared to leave things to chance and Elvin and Hoskins decided to take their riders away for some 'team bonding', as it would now be called. The rest cure, as it was called then, took place 'somewhere near Folkestone'. Hoskins told the press that he had barred all luxuries such as motoring and late hours. 'The boys are forbidden to drive motor cycles or motor cars,' he said, 'or even to look at them. Their bed time is 10.30 p.m. sharp!' Their diet was carefully chosen by Wembley's physical instructor, Mr Tyler, and games, swimming and physical jerks were not only encouraged but rigidly enforced. He thought this would restore physical fitness to the team and enable them to make 'strenuous efforts' for big honours. He also hoped that the rest cure would help some of the riders mentally. Van Praag, for example, was languishing in the reserves when he should have been one of the Lions' leading scorers. Hoskins put his loss of form down to a bad fall he'd had at Stamford Bridge earlier in the season. This had snapped his nerves.

At the end of their two weeks 'somewhere near Folkestone', Hoskins declared, 'All the boys are looking fine. There isn't the slightest doubt that this fortnight's rest cure has done them the world of good.'

As well as their physical and mental well-being, Elvin and Hoskins also decided they needed to look after their bikes' mechanical well-being. And so, following much lobbying by their New Zealand star Wally Kilmister, who attributed his success back in his own country to having such a facility available, they introduced a test bed for the machines in the Wembley workshop, built by Kilmister himself. It meant that all the team members could test their bikes without having to set wheel on the track itself. This was a great innovation and enabled the riders and mechanics to set up full-scale tests whenever they wanted.

The first round of the National Trophy was next, with a home tie against Stamford Bridge. Watson was back to partner Byers. Ormston was missing through injury, so Lees stood in as captain. Things were neck and neck up to heat seven, but then Kilmister and Whitfield forced themselves past Dicky Smythe to take a 5-1. Two further 5-1s followed in heats ten and eleven. Heat twelve was a cracking heat as Evans shot away from the start, only to be taken by Gus Kuhn coming out of the second bend. Wal Phillips then joined Kuhn in front as he dived under Evans, giving the Pensioners a 5-1 position. But Evans was not beaten and he found a way past the Bridge pair with a daredevil round-the-boards effort. But he couldn't shake off Phillips, who stuck to him like glue as they roared into the last lap neck and neck. Coming round the final bend, Phillips went high then cut down on the inside to surprise Evans and regain the lead, just retaining it on the run-in by inches. In the meantime, the other Wembley rider, Greenwood, had managed to get past Kuhn to make the heat a 3-3. At the end of the evening, Wembley had a 12-point lead (54-42) to take in the second leg at Stamford Bridge.

The absence of their captain, Gus Kuhn, did not help the Pensioners in the second leg but, for Wembley, there was a return to form for Watson and although Stamford Bridge just managed to scrape a one-point win in the match, 46-45, they lost on aggregate 99-88. It was a bad-tempered match with the steward called upon to make several decisions following 'hard' riding. In heat thirteen he excluded Watson after four laps of clashes, bumping and boring between him and the Pensioners' Charlie Blacklock. This decision did not go down well with the Wembley supporters in the crowd, and fights broke out on the terraces while stones and bottles were thrown at Watson by the Stamford Bridge supporters.

The away match at Clapton on 10 August saw Reg Bounds badly injured in a fall, suffering severe concussion. He was unconscious and on the danger list for a number of days and, even when he was out of danger, it seemed he would be out of racing for the rest of the season.

Shortly after this there was a change in the Wembley management as Johnnie Hoskins left to take over as manager at Elvin's other team, West Ham. In his place came Alec Jackson. Jackson had been a pioneer rider in the North of England, taking part in the first ever meeting in Manchester, at Audenshaw on 3 March 1928, as well as the first meeting at Belle Vue (Kirkmanshulme Lane) on 28 July 1928. Succeeding the incomparable Johnnie Hoskins might have seemed a daunting task to most, but Jackson saw it as a great challenge, a challenge he was to relish, so much so that he was to become arguably the greatest manager of all time.

Jackson was also able to match Hoskins in flair and showmanship. He believed in continuing the Hoskins tradition of putting on interval displays that alone would be worth the admission money. Just some of the events he later lined up were motorcycle acrobatic displays by the Royal Army Signal Corps; Eric Peacock, the one-armed trick cyclist; Chasewater Charlie, the 'cyclownatic'; the 'death-defying "Cyclone" Danny Carter' leaping through a flaming glass building and Duffy and Pearl, the 'World's Wonders on Wheels'. One event that didn't go down

Alec Jackson.

too well with Sir Arthur Elvin was when he invited the well-known American stunt rider, Putt Mossman, to put on an interval display. Mossman decided to perform, as his finale, a motorcycle striptease act. Standing on the saddle of his bike he removed his jacket, shirt and trousers. He appeared to be standing on his bike naked, although he was, in fact, wearing a skin-coloured pair of briefs. The next day, when he went to collect his money, the straight-laced Elvin told him he was banned from ever appearing at Wembley again.

Jackson's first move was to make a thorough inspection of all the team's machinery, as he felt they were underpowered. He ordered that all the bikes be taken away for testing at their new test facility. The testing was still taking place when the Lions were due to race their next match the following evening, at home to Plymouth, so the whole team were forced to ride their number two bikes or on borrowed equipment. Fortunately they were still able to beat a weak Plymouth side by 27 to 24.

The London Cup semi-final against Crystal Palace followed. With their bikes now at full power, the Lions crushed the opposition 65-30. All the Wembley team seemed to be on top form that evening. Lees broke the track record and Kilmister scored a maximum while Ormston and Greenwood contributed 9 each. For the Palace, only Johnson put up any sort of show, with 10 points. Even Farndon could only manage 5 against the rampant Lions. The Glaziers put up a much better show in the second leg on their own track. Johnson scored 12 and Farndon and Joe Francis weighed in with 11 each, but it was not quite good enough and a 56-37 win for Crystal Palace meant the semi-final went to Wembley by 102 to 86.

After the short interlude for cup matches, Wembley returned to the league and were beginning to prove almost invincible. Even the strong Belle Vue Aces suffered a humiliating 41-13 defeat at the Empire Stadium on 25 August. However, just two days later, in the return encounter at Hyde Road, the tables were turned and the Lions suffered their first league defeat in eight matches when they went down 29-25.

The National Trophy semi-final was next on the agenda for Wembley, but it turned out to be an easy victory as they first of all demolished Coventry by 18 points at Brandon and then in the second leg on their home track by 30 points. The winning margin was 119-71.

Shortly after this, Jackson announced that although Reg Bounds had now left hospital he would definitely be out for the rest of the season. His condition had been extremely serious and he needed at least six months to recuperate.

With the Test series for the Ashes this year finely balanced at 2-2, much interest was shown in the fifth and final deciding match. This was due to take place on Clapton's track at Lea Bridge, but Elvin stepped in with an offer to run the match at Wembley in order to accommodate the number of spectators expected. Having been guaranteed half the gross gate with a minimum of £1,000, the Clapton management readily accepted the change of venue. Admission prices were set at 10s 6d, 5s, 2s 6d and 1s 3d for 18 September.

As it turned out, the £1,000 minimum was to prove totally unnecessary as not only Londoners but supporters from all over the country descended on the Empire Stadium. Although they had expected a good gate, the Wembley management were taken aback by the numbers who eventually came. Thousands upon thousands fought their way to the turnstiles and terraces, climbing over one another's shoulders in an effort to force their way in. Police reinforcements were called for and these too were overwhelmed in the biggest rush speedway had ever seen. A huge traffic jam extended well down the Harrow Road and motorists abandoned their cars miles from the stadium.

And so, on a sweltering hot evening, something like 70,000 people packed into the Empire Stadium to see this deciding Test match, a record for a speedway meeting at that time. The BBC broadcast the match live on the radio and Pathé News made a film of the match to be shown in cinemas around the country.

The atmosphere was electric throughout the match, which was fought out through one continuous roar of cheering from the spectators. Riding like a man inspired, Vic Huxley proved to be the Man of the Match, scoring a maximum, but it wasn't enough to prevent the Aussies going down by 51 points to 42. There was much satisfaction for the home supporters too, as Lees proved to be the best Englishman, top scoring with 10 points, equal to Belle Vue's Eric Langton.

This brought to an end a successful international year for the Lions. Lees had appeared in four Tests for England, top scoring in two; Greenwood had ridden in three, top scoring in one while Watson, Ormston and Byers had all ridden in one each. In addition, Van Praag had ridden in three for Australia. Six Wembley riders had therefore represented their countries during the course of the season. The only other regular team member, Wally Kilmister, was the New Zealand champion. It was little wonder that Wembley were now carrying all before them in the National League, the National Trophy and the London Cup.

The next big meeting of the season also took place at the Empire Stadium as Wembley staged the final of the Star Riders' Championship. In contrast to the heat of Test match night, the Star final was run on a cold, wet evening. Once again, each team was represented by two riders,

George Greenwood.

Wembley's pair being Lees and Byers. Unfortunately, neither of them made the final run-off, which was won by Langton from Huxley, with Case in third place.

Back to team business the following week, the Lions found themselves away to Stamford Bridge in the first leg of the London Cup final. It was a close-run affair, with Wembley just losing by one point. In the return leg the scores remained level until heat ten, but the Lions did just enough to ensure victory by six points and therefore the tie by five. Heat fifteen saw one of the best races of the season as Kilmister and Stamford Bridge's Jack Chapman fought it out for four laps. Their two riding styles were in sharp contrast. Whereas Kilmister was the all-action do-or-die type, Chapman was a smooth stylist. They passed and repassed with Kilmister changing line, first on the outside, then down on the inside, sometimes abruptly cutting across Chapman but always giving him room. Chapman, meanwhile, held to his line and kept coming back at Kilmister, never giving up, but it was the Wembley rider who did just enough to win by a length. Although the Pensioners had three outstanding riders in Wal Phillips, who scored a maximum, Frank Arthur and Dicky Smythe, Wembley were more solid overall, with Lees scoring 10, Whitfield 9 and Ormston, Evans and Byers 7 each. The London Cup was presented to the Lions by Mr Orley of the *London Evening News*.

Next on Wembley's agenda was the National League title, with a double header taking place on 6 October. The first match was a crucial one as the Lions were currently top of the league, with their opponents in the match, Crystal Palace, currently occupying the runners-up spot.

After eight heats the scores were all level at 24 each. The Lions were represented in the last heat by Greenwood and Kilmister, while the Glaziers tracked Tom Farndon and Alec Peel.

Unfortunately for Wembley, it was Farndon who flew off from the start and established a commanding lead. Greenwood and Kilmister packed in behind and it looked as though the match would end in a draw but, dramatically, Farndon overdid it on the last lap and fell, leaving Greenwood to take the chequered flag with Kilmister in second place and a 5-1 heat win to give Wembley the match by 29 points to 25.

The second match of the evening was against Coventry and, once again, the Lions looked far from league leaders as they made heavy weather of the match, again forcing a win in the last heat. Although it was hard going, these two wins proved enough to give Wembley the league championship by three points.

The following week, the Lions took on Belle Vue in the first leg of the National Trophy final. This time they rode much better and hammered the Aces by 66 points to 29, giving them a cushion of 37 points to take away to Manchester. It was to prove enough as, although the Lions lost by 21 points, they claimed the last leg of the treble by 103 points to 87.

The Empire Stadium closed its doors on speedway for the season with a challenge match against Australia, which Wembley won by 28 to 26 after nine heats. Although rain forced the abandonment of the rest of the meeting, it did not stop the presentation of the league and cup trophies. Major Percy Davies, deputy editor of the *News of the World*, presented the league trophy and a cheque for £140 while Tom Stenner of the *Daily Mail* presented the National Trophy and gold medals to each individual member of the team.

It had been a fantastically successful year for the Lions. They had won the league title for the third year in succession and had also pulled off the treble, a feat so far unique in speedway history.

Incidentally, it was a sign of the times that the three major trophies in speedway were sponsored by national newspapers who gave as much coverage as possible to the events.

The Lions had now reached the apex of the domestic speedway world. Was the only way left for them down?

1932 National Association Trophy Averages – qualification 6 matches

	Matches	Rides	Points	CMA
Ginger Lees	18	54	114	8.44
Jack Ormston	16	48	86	7.17
George Greenwood	16	48	84	7.00
Reg Bounds	13	39	59	6.05
Lionel Van Praag	9	27	27	5.93
Harry Whitfield	15	45	63	5.60
Gordon Byers	6	18	24	5.33
Colin Watson	13	39	51	5.23

National League Averages – qualification 6 matches

	Matches	Rides	Points	CMA
Ginger Lees	16	48	118	10.25
Gordon Byers	14	42	70	8.29

Wally Kilmister	16	48	88	8.08
Harry Whitfield	8	24	36	7.27
George Greenwood	10	30	47	6.90
Jack Ormston	14	42	56	6.57
Lionel Van Praag	7	21	30	5.71
Colin Watson	7	21	26	4.95
Norman Evans	8	24	24	4.00

National Association Trophy matches

Date	H/A	Against	W/L/D	Score
13 April	Away	Southampton	Won	29-24
19 April	Away	Plymouth	Won	36-15
28 April	Home	Stamford Bridge	Won	31-21
30 April	Away	Crystal Palace	Lost	26-27
5 May	Home	Wimbledon	Won	28-24
7 May	Away	Belle Vue	Lost	25-29
12 May	Home	Southampton	Won	37-16
19 May	Home	Coventry	Won	33-20
25 May	Away	Sheffield	Won	34-20
26 May	Home	Plymouth	Won	36-16
2 June	Home	Crystal Palace	Won	32-22
7 June	Away	West Ham	Won	29-25
9 June	Home	Belle Vue	Won	28-25
20 June	Away	Wimbledon	Lost	26-28
30 June	Home	Sheffield	Won	41-11
2 July	Away	Coventry	Won	34-20
6 July	Away	Stamford Bridge	Lost	17-37
7 July	Home	West Ham	Won	31-23

National Association Trophy Table

	Played	Won	Drawn	Lost	For	Against	Points
Stamford Bridge	18	16	0	2	587	374	32
WEMBLEY	18	14	0	4	553	403	28
Crystal Palace	18	12	0	6	522	436	24
Belle Vue	18	11	0	7	548	411	22
West Ham	18	11	0	7	505.5	446.5	22
Wimbledon	18	11	0	7	485	456	22
Southampton/Clapton	18	5	0	13	417	533	10
Coventry	18	5	0	13	401.5	547.5	10
Sheffield	18	3	0	15	371	574	6
Plymouth	18	2	0	16	364	573	4

National League Matches

Date	H/A	Against	W/L/D	Score
14 July	Home	Clapton	Won	33-20
21 July	Home	Wimbledon	Won	29-25
26 July	Away	Plymouth	Won	35-16
1 August	Away	Coventry	Won	29-22
10 August	Away	Clapton	Won	34-20
11 August	Home	Plymouth	Won	27-24
25 August	Home	Belle Vue	Won	41-13
27 August	Away	Belle Vue	Lost	25-29
1 September	Home	Stamford Bridge	Won	30-24
8 September	Home	West Ham	Won	33-20
20 September	Away	West Ham	Won	40-14
24 September	Away	Crystal Palace	Lost	24-30
26 September	Away	Wimbledon	Won	31-23
1 October	Away	Stamford Bridge	Lost	25-29
6 October	Home	Crystal Palace	Won	29-25
6 October	Home	Coventry	Won	30-24

National League Table

	Played	Won	Drawn	Lost	For	Against	Points
WEMBLEY	16	13	0	3	495	358	26
Crystal Palace	16	11	1	4	467	386	23
Belle Vue	16	9	1	6	452.5	393.5	19
Stamford Bridge	16	8	1	7	467	389	17
Wimbledon	16	8	1	7	427.5	425.5	17
West Ham	16	7	0	9	397	447	14
Coventry	16	6	0	10	384.5	463.5	12
Clapton	16	4	0	12	370	479	8
Plymouth	16	4	0	12	356.5	475.5	8

National Trophy

First Round
Wembley: Bye

Second Round
Wembley 54 Stamford Bridge 42
Stamford Bridge 46 Wembley 45
Aggregate: Wembley 99 Stamford Bridge 88

Semi-Final
Wembley 63 Coventry 33
Coventry 38 Wembley 56
Aggregate: Wembley 119 Coventry 71

Final
Wembley 66 Belle Vue 29
Belle Vue 58 Wembley 37
Aggregate: Wembley 103 Belle Vue 87

London Cup

First Round
Wembley: Bye

Semi-Final
Wembley 65 Crystal Palace 30
Crystal Palace 56 Wembley 37
Aggregate: Wembley 102 Crystal Palace 86

Final
Wembley 52 Stamford Bridge 44
Stamford Bridge 48 Wembley 47
Aggregate: Wembley 99 Stamford Bridge 92

SIX

1933 – THE BUBBLE BURSTS

Wembley's opening night in 1933 was 11 May, just five days after the Rugby League Challenge Cup final. Between the Saturday and the Thursday, 2,000 square yards of turf had to be removed from the outer portions of the football field and replaced with 400 tons of cinders. But that was just the start of Wembley's problems. As from 8 May, a new starting procedure was introduced. Until then, all races had been started with a rolling start. The riders did a lap of the track and then, coming up to the starting line, they were supposed to get roughly in line as the starting marshal waved the green flag to signify the start of the race. This method of starting led to many false starts as riders tried to get a slight advantage by speeding up a little as they came to the line. The new clutch-start method meant there would be no more preliminary lap and the riders would come up to the start line and stay still while the red light was on. The starter would then signal the start of the race with a green light instead of a flag. Any rider experiencing a mechanical problem would be allowed two minutes to rectify it. After the red light came on, any rider stalling his engine had to wait until the green light, at which time he could be pushed off as far as the thirty-yard forward foul line.

This new method of starting meant that tracks had to reinforce the home straights around the starting area to counteract the effect of the rear wheels digging into the track when the riders let their clutches out. So the Wembley management now had to lay down 250 yards of special quick-drying cement along the home straight as well as all the other work. The concrete base extended to a depth of six inches before being covered up with cinders.

In addition to work on the track, Arthur Elvin also doubled the volume of floodlighting around the track to forty lamp standards with a total capacity of 160,000 candle power, making Wembley the best-lit track in the country. The origin of this improvement dated back to the film that was taken of the Test match, when the track had had to be specially lit for the occasion. Elvin was so impressed that he decided to upgrade the general lighting to that standard.

As far as the team went, Wembley had no intention of breaking up their treble-winning formation and retained Watson, Lees, Whitfield, Byers, Bounds, Kilmister, Evans and Parkinson. Ormston was missing, as he had decided to stay in America, and so Watson was reappointed captain.

Apart from Ormston's non-return there was one other snag in retaining the same team, as the control board had decided to introduce a measure of rider control in an attempt to even up the teams so that, in theory, any team could win the league. The first new rule they introduced was

Gordon Byers.

that any rider appearing on a team's retained list could not be transferred to another team without the approval of both promoters and the control board. Any rider that was transferred before 1 June would go on a free transfer and after that date transfer fees were permissible up to a limit of £500. The idea of this was to stop the richer teams being able to snap up all the best riders.

Wembley's policy of importing ready-made stars, which had paid such handsome dividends, was now no longer possible and so Jackson looked to training up his own riders and organised trials. Out of forty novices who started out, Jackson selected twelve who he thought had the makings of speedway riders for further trials. It was this new policy of training up his own riders that would in time make Jackson the most successful speedway manager of all time.

However, it was the second new rule that really affected Wembley. According to this rule, any rider not in the country over the close season, even if they appeared on a team's retained list, would become the 'property' of the control board and could be allocated to any team on their return. Wembley had two riders out in Australia over the winter of 1932/33, Van Praag and Shelton. The control board ruled that Wembley could retain the services of only one of these riders, while the other was allocated to Nottingham. Elvin and Jackson were desperate to keep the services of Van Praag, who they saw as a much better bet for the future than Shelton, and they were fortunately able to persuade the Nottingham management that they should take Shelton. Shelton had been the Nottingham captain before his transfer to Wembley, so they were quite happy to have him back.

One rider appearing on Belle Vue's retained list for the first time was a young rider by the name of Bill Kitchen. He was well known in northern motorcycling circles as a trials and grass track rider, but this was to be his first taste of speedway. Many years later, when he had established himself as one of the top stars of the sport, Kitchen was to become the Wembley captain.

Ten teams entered the National League in 1933, those being Belle Vue, Clapton, Coventry, Crystal Palace, Nottingham, Plymouth, Sheffield, Wembley, West Ham and Wimbledon. Scoring returned to the old 4-2-1 system. The theory behind this change was that it now made it necessary for at least one man on each side to go all-out for first place, which in turn would lead to more spectacular racing.

Before opening night at the Empire Stadium a couple of the Wembley riders had some individual successes. Lees won the Wimbledon Championship for the second year running, while Kilmister became the first New Zealander to obtain a Gold Star for lapping Brooklands at over 100mph with an ordinary speedway engine.

The team rode in two matches before opening night. The first was at Coventry, where Lees continued his good form, scoring a paid maximum in his team's 34-27 victory. The second match proved to be a disaster for the Lions, and perhaps an early indication that this season was not going to be as successful as the last, as West Ham annihilated them by 46.5 to 16.5. It was the first time the Hammers had ever beaten their sister track, out-pointing Wembley in every heat, and was the Lions' biggest defeat ever. Hero of the night for West Ham was Bluey Wilkinson, who scored a maximum.

This poor form looked like continuing on Wembley's opening night as, after four heats, they found themselves 10 points down to Crystal Palace. Although the Glaziers scored a 4-3 in the fourth heat, this seemed to be the turning point of the match as Crystal Palace captain Ron Johnson was excluded for starting before the green light came on. Even though Joe Francis won the race for Crystal Palace, this incident seemed to affect their starting as they made sure there would be no more exclusions. Newton was left at the start in heat five, while the same thing happened to the normally fast-starting Tom Farndon in heat six. As a result, Wembley gained two 6-1s in these heats to pull back the deficit. In the end it was a good victory for the Lions by 34 points to 29.

There was another victory at Wimbledon four days later through some solid teamwork, with Kilmister and Van Praag scoring 8 points and Lees, Byers and Evans each contributing 6. Wembley ran out winners by 38 to 25.

Just when the nightmare of the West Ham match seemed to be behind them, Wembley suffered another disastrous defeat, this time at the hands of Clapton. Jack Parker was in immaculate form for the home team, beating the Wembley riders out of the start every time as though they were novices and leading his team to a 44-18 victory.

Away to one of the league's unfashionable teams in their next match, it was expected that Wembley would bounce back from this defeat. But it was not be as they lost 34-29 to Plymouth. The warning bells were definitely starting to ring for the team that had carried all before them the previous season.

Back home at the Empire Stadium on 18 May, Wembley were able to defeat a strong Belle Vue team. Lees in particular was in good form, beating Langton in heat two in a new clutch-start track record of 79.6 seconds. Langton's laconic response as he returned to the pits after the race was, 'He was going too fast for me.' Belle Vue's newcomer, Bill Kitchen, showed up well on his first visit to Wembley, scoring 8 points. His performance in the last heat of the match was particularly noteworthy as he got out of the start behind the top Lions pair Lees and Van Praag, but managed to get past Van Praag to take second place. The final score was Wembley 38 Belle Vue 23.

The following week however, saw another poor performance by Wembley, as they lost at home to Wimbledon by 37 points to 25. The Dons' Claude Rye scored a maximum, knocking a whole second off the track record in heat two. Huxley also scored a maximum. Wembley's only heat win of the night came in heat six as Watson and Byers scored a 6-1.

The league table as at 30 May showed Wembley in a very unaccustomed sixth position, with just 8 points from 8 matches. Clapton were top with 16 from 9.

An eventful match at Nottingham on 5 June saw the Lions back on top form as they whipped their opponents 45-16. The match had started off well for the Outlaws. Their captain, Strecker, riding brilliantly, smashed his own track record in the first heat. Heat two saw Lees and former Lion Shelton both excluded for jumping the start. The two New Zealanders, Kilmister for Wembley and Charlie Blacklock for Nottingham, seemed to have their own private battle going in heat three as they came together several times. In the end it was Blacklock who left the track and fell, leaving Kilmister to take the four points. At the end of heat seven, with two heats to go, Wembley had gone into a small lead, 26-22. But with four points for a win, it was still anybody's match, until the ludicrous events of heat eight. In that heat, Strecker, Chapman and Van Praag were all excluded for jumping the start and Lees was left to go on a lonely tour of the track. The steward's decision was anything but popular, particularly as with this race went Nottingham's chance of victory.

There was much booing and jeering from all parts of the stadium and protests from both team managements. After a long delay the ninth heat was eventually raced and won by Kilmister, who thus took maximum points for the match. Riding with Whitfield, the pair only dropped one point and were mainly responsible for the Lions' return to winning ways.

The sort of farce that had resulted in only one rider taking part in heat eight was to some extent being replayed at stadia all over the country. To combat this disease of jumping the light, the Crystal Palace management, under their promoter Fred Mockford, had experimented with the introduction of a starting gate. The experiment had proved successful and the control board ruled that in future all tracks were to install starting gates. Only three weeks were allowed from the date of the ruling, 20 June, before it became obligatory. A supplementary rule said, 'Any rider touching the tapes is to be sent back and, upon repeating the offence, is to be excluded from the race.' It was reckoned that the cost of installing a starting gate would be less than £5, including labour charges.

Although Jackson was still keen on training up his juniors, he realised that something drastic had to be done to move Wembley up the table, so he put in a request to transfer the Australian Test rider Dicky Case from Coventry. As Coventry were doing even worse than Wembley, the control board refused to sanction the move and Case stayed at Brandon.

Wembley's next home match had to be abandoned after heat eight. The start had been delayed by half an hour because of rain and when it did start there were pools of water all over the track. What followed was described by one commentator as 'speedway without the speed'. Conditions got worse and worse and just as the riders were coming up to the line for the last heat a torrential downpour of such intensity that racing was out of the question fell. The meeting was abandoned with the scores standing at Wembley 38 Sheffield 17. Both managers agreed that the match should be awarded to Wembley, who were in an impregnable position. Unfortunately for Jackson and his Lions, the control board refused to allow it and ordered a re-run.

It wasn't just at speedway that Wembley seemed to be having no luck. In a golf match against the Press, the Lions lost 4-2 with two halved. Only Kilmister and Van Praag won their matches.

The poor run continued as the Lions found themselves to be no match for a very much in-form Crystal Palace team, losing 39-23. It was left to Lees to salvage a bit of pride, scoring 10 points.

Although they won their next match at home, beating West Ham by 38 points to 24, the bad luck stayed with them as, following an incident when Van Praag appeared to put Tommy Allott into the fence, he was severely reprimanded and fined £15. Nevertheless, it was a greatly improved performance from Wembley; Kilmister rode brilliantly for a maximum, while Lees dropped just one point to Wilkinson.

The second half of this match saw the Lions take on a Danish touring team. It proved to be no contest as Wembley thrashed the visitors by 22 points to 6. Only West Ham's Morian Hansen put up any form of resistance.

At about this time a new Gaumont musical film was being shot, called *Britannia of Billingsgate*, starring Gordon Harker, Violet Loraine and a very young John Mills. Part of the story called for some speedway action and among those riders signed up to film the relevant scenes was Wembley's Colin Watson.

Although Wembley had managed to win their encounter with West Ham, Jackson moved into the transfer market to try and strengthen his team. His choice of rider, however, did not meet with universal acclaim from the supporters and seemed to many to be a strange choice. The rider he brought in was Percy Dunn, who already in his short career had been attached to Middlesbrough, Newcastle, Belle Vue, Glasgow and Stamford Bridge. Jackson believed he had potential and that all he needed was a suitable opportunity and a little encouragement. Unfortunately it appears that Jackson's critics were right on this one and Jackson wrong, as Percy Dunn seems to have sunk without trace after signing for the Lions.

The next meeting at the Empire Stadium was the first Test match of the year, won convincingly by England 76-47. Lees beat Huxley twice and finished up as England's top scorer with the best ever Test score of 20 points, thanks to the four points for a first place rule.

The following week it seemed that Wembley were back to their best as they defeated Plymouth 46-17 – and that was after a 6-1 reverse in the first heat. Lees and Van Praag were the outstanding pair, recording 6-1s in all three of their heats.

In spite of this return to form, the league table as at 11 July did not make happy reading for the Lions' supporters, who were so used to success. Belle Vue were top with 28 points from 18 matches, while Wembley were still languishing in sixth place with 20 points from 17 matches.

In the second Test match at Belle Vue, Lees rode even better than in the first, top scoring for England with 22 points. To this day that is still the highest number of points scored by one individual in a Test match. It was not enough to stop England losing by 65 points to 61, however.

Lees and Van Praag were once again unbeaten in Wembley's next home match on 13 July, scoring 18 points between them and helping their team to a 49.5-13.5 demolition of Clapton. Byers, Kilmister and Lees all scored full maximums. Although Lees was running into the best form of his life, it was a guest performer who took the evening's plaudits as Belle Vue's Bill Kitchen equalled Watson's 'Cinders' record of 19.0 seconds, which had stood since May 1931. Lees had a go but failed to equal or beat the record.

A pre-war view of the stadium on match night.

With the improvement in form of their top riders, the Lions seemed to be getting back to something like their 1932 form and, in their next match, a National Trophy first round first leg tie away at Nottingham, they crushed the opposition 79-44. Lees scored 22, Watson 18 and Kilmister 16, including one exclusion.

The Lions then went on to record yet another win in the replayed National League match against Nottingham. This time the rain held off and Wembley ran out victors by 37 points to 26. It was Kilmister's turn to score a maximum, while Lees and Byers contributed 8 each.

At the beginning of August the traffic commissioner announced a restriction on the number of coaches that were allowed to take supporters of sports clubs to away fixtures. In some cases the commissioner refused to grant any licenses at all. In response, Wembley issued a press bulletin that said, 'Hundreds of enthusiasts are being prevented from attending meetings, both in London and in the country.' They vowed to take up the fight on behalf of their supporters and all speedway fans throughout the country.

For their third match in succession against Nottingham, this time in the second leg of the National Trophy first round, the Lions put on a dazzling display, crushing the Outlaws by 103 points to 22. Fourteen out of the eighteen heats were won by a maximum 6-1. Lees scored 20 points from five rides, Kilmister 18 from five, Byers 16 from five and Watson 14 from five. So far in front were Wembley that none of these riders not bothered to take their final ride and were replaced by the Lions' reserves. The *Speedway News* reported that, 'Times, on the whole, were exceptionally slow, but there was nothing to make the winners hurry.' The final aggregate score was Wembley 182 Nottingham 66.

Wembley's revival continued as, in their next match, they beat West Ham 66-60 away in their London Cup semi-final first leg tie. Unfortunately it came at a price, as top scorer on the night, Kilmister, hit a bump in the track and fell in his last ride, breaking his collarbone. He had scored 14 points. Lees was second highest with 13.

The loss of Kilmister for a few matches was a big blow to Wembley as he had been riding exceptionally well at the time and was the Lions' highest-placed rider in the National League averages with cma of 8.63 (based on three rides per match and four points for a win). Top was Clapton's Jack Parker with a cma of 9.70. The next highest Wembley rider was Lees, who was in thirteenth place with an average of 7.47.

Kilmister was forced to watch the second leg of the London Cup semi-final from the stands with his arm in a sling, but at least he had the satisfaction of seeing his team beat the Hammers by 77 points to 46 and take the tie on aggregate 143-106. Man of the Match was Byers, who scored 20 points, with Whitfield taking 17.

Wembley's next match, a National League match away at Coventry, was not raced under the best of circumstances. The Brandon track was in a dreadful state and several Wembley supporters expressed their opinion of it quite forcibly by climbing the fence and staging a sit-down on the track. They were eventually removed by the police and the match went ahead. Van Praag was brought back into the team to replace Kilmister and proved to be the Lions' best rider on the night, though that wasn't difficult as the team in general could not get to grips with the track, losing by 42 points to 21.

The next home meeting proved to be a very exciting affair as Wembley took on Clapton on 10 August. Kilmister's absence was matched by that of Norman Parker for the Lea Bridge side and there were never more than three points between the two teams. The good news for Wembley was that Bounds was able to make a comeback for the team exactly one year to the day after his accident – and against the same team. Going into the last heat, Wembley led by a single point, 28-27, but it was Clapton's Phil Bishop who shot off from the start and never looked like being headed. In an amazing fairytale ending, Bounds proved to be the Lions' hero. For four laps, he was in last place behind Roy Barrowclough. This would have given Clapton a 5-2 and victory in the match, but just on the last bend, Bounds put in one last desperate effort and managed to pass the Clapton rider to turn the 5-2 in to a 4-3 and change the defeat into a 31-31 draw.

In the second half, Wembley held their Star Championship eliminating round to find their two riders for the final. Unfortunately, neither of their best two riders were able to take part. Kilmister, of course, was suffering from his broken collarbone while Lees had injured his ankle during the Clapton match. This left Whitfield and Watson to come first and second and thus become Wembley's representatives in the final.

Although Lees had been unable to take part in the second half, he was back fully fit for Wembley's next match away to Clapton, top scoring with 7 points, but it was not enough to prevent a Clapton win by 34 to 28.

Lees' next appearance was in the fourth Test at Wimbledon. For the third time that season, Lees was England's top scorer with 17 points. It was the closest Test so far, resulting in a narrow two-point win for Australia, 64-62.

In spite of Wembley's inconsistent form, they managed to reach the final of the National Trophy, beating Crystal Palace in the semi-final by the aggregate score of 140-110. For the first leg at home, Watson was reappointed Lions captain and was back to his best form, scoring 19 points. His spectacular leg-trailing style proved inspirational as he rode all his races round the outside, passing the opposition in great sweeps on the bends. Lees and Whitfield gave him strong support, scoring 16 each, enabling Wembley to take a commanding lead from the first leg, 77-48. The second leg back at Sydenham proved to be an evenly balanced contest with the final score being 63-62 to the Lions.

Wembley were now in two cup finals, the National Trophy and the London Cup, but were still floundering in sixth place in the National League with 25 points from 22 matches, while leaders Belle Vue had 42 from 25.

Before either of the cup finals could take place, Wembley hosted a major individual championship, the Wembley Silver Cup. Most of the league's top riders took part, including Bluey Wilkinson, Ron Johnson, Vic Huxley, Tom Farndon, Tiger Stevenson and all the Wembley team. In spite of the wealth of talent on show, three Wembley riders, Lees, Kilmister and Whitfield, made the final, along with Wilkinson. The final saw Lees take the cup from Kilmister with Wilkinson in third place.

The first leg of the first of the cup finals, the London Cup, took place on 28 August at Wimbledon. The Lions put on a magnificent performance for the occasion. The big factor in their 71-53 away victory was the continued great form of their captain, Watson. Watson had looked very dejected before the match started, saying that the game was 'getting too tough' for him now. Five wins and 20 points showed that he had made this statement with his tongue firmly in his cheek. Kilmister was back for this match and immediately returned to form, scoring 19. Lees was going well, scoring 11 points before a collision with Wimbledon's Geoff Pymar, who tried to get through a gap that didn't exist, put him out for the rest of the evening.

As in the first leg, Wembley owed their victory in the second leg of the London Cup over Wimbledon, by 69 points to 56, to their rejuvenated captain Colin Watson, who scored 18 points. But that brief statement does not do full justice to his performance that night. In the first heat of the match his chain broke in three pieces with one portion inflicting a severe gash on the inside of his leg. Despite this, he turned out in his remaining heats as though nothing had happened and was undefeated by an opponent for the rest of the evening. Wembley's London Cup triumph owed much to Watson's performance in both legs of the final. Another rider who had been suffering from loss of form also pulled through for the team as Whitfield top scored with 20 points. The final aggregate victory of 140-109 was all the more worthy as Lees had still not recovered from the ankle injury sustained in the first leg and took no part in the second.

Although they had managed a fine cup win, Wembley continued to struggle in the league as they lost their next two matches, home to Wimbledon and away at Plymouth. However, they did have a good excuse in both as Lees was still unable to take part and Watson had suffered concussion riding for England in the fifth Test at West Ham after scoring 9 points and was also absent from both matches.

The next meeting at Wembley was the 1933 Star Riders' Championship final. With Lees and Kilmister already out and Watson also unable to take part due to injury, the Lions' hopes rested on Whitfield. But it was not to be. Although he reached the semi-final, he came third and was eliminated from the meeting. The winner was the young Crystal Palace phenomenon Tom Farndon, who was just beginning to move into the ranks of the true superstars of the sport.

As it happened, Wembley were up against Crystal Palace in their next league match. Farndon showed them why he was the Star Riders Champion by scoring a flawless maximum. Watson returned for this match but could only manage 1 point as the Lions crashed 42-21.

A further defeat at the hands of West Ham followed, making it four consecutive league defeats for Wembley. It was now the middle of September and time was running out for the Lions as far as league honours went. They were still in sixth place, 23 points behind the leaders Belle Vue, with just two matches in hand.

Colin Watson.

To get through the outstanding fixtures, Wembley began a series of double-headers. The first was on 21 September, when they took on Crystal Palace and Sheffield. The team rode well in the first match to defeat the Glaziers by 35 points to 27, Kilmister managing to inflict a defeat on Farndon in the last heat. The second match turned into a rout as Wembley recorded seven 6-1s, with Watson and Byers undefeated as a pair. The final score was Wembley 51 Sheffield 12.

Although they had won these two league matches, Wembley's realistic last hope of a national honour rested in their next two matches, the two legs of the National Trophy final against league leaders Belle Vue.

The first leg was held on 28 September at the Empire Stadium. Unfortunately for the Lions, Lees was still unable to ride and Watson, although taking part, was far from match fit. From the very first heat, when the England and Belle Vue star Eric Langton equalled the track record (78.6 seconds), the crowd knew it was going to be a hopeless task for their beloved Lions. In the first half of the match only two of the team, Kilmister and Whitfield, showed any fight. To make matters worse, Whitfield was brought down in his first race after the interval and was ruled out not only for the rest of the evening but for the return leg as well. Van Praag seemed to get going after the interval, scoring two wins and a third place after scoring nothing in the first half. Kilmister was far and away the top scorer for Wembley with 18 points; Whitfield managed 10. For the Aces, Langton scored a fine paid maximum while Varey contributed 13 points as Langton's partner. Abbott and Kitchen, the other two heat leaders, each scored 14.

And so Wembley had to take a deficit of 18 points to Hyde Road, having lost 54-72. It looked a hopeless task and so it proved, but the nature of the crushing defeat was so overwhelming that it took everyone by surprise.

Belle Vue's biggest crowd of all time turned out to see their heroes in the cup final. The start was delayed by half an hour while the last of some 40,000 people were crammed into the stadium. Even so, there were hundreds left outside when the gates were finally closed. In the match itself, the Langton/Varey partnership alone scored more points than the entire Wembley team and would have gone through the match undefeated as a pair had not Varey suffered from engine failure in the tenth race. Kilmister was the only Lion to extend the victorious Aces in the first half, although, as in the first leg, Van Praag seemed to wake up after the interval to score two race wins. In the end he finished as top scorer for Wembley with 11 points, Kilmister coming second with 9. The contrast with the Belle Vue team could hardly have been greater as Varey weighed in with 18, Abbott 17, Langton 16 and Grosskreutz 15. The final score was Belle Vue 92 Wembley 33, making the aggregate score 164-87. It was the first time the National Trophy had left London. And with Belle Vue's unassailable lead in the National League, a new era of dominance by the Manchester team was ushered in that night. Wembley's reign was over.

In spite of this heavy defeat and the fact there was nothing really left for Wembley, they bounced back with an away victory over Wimbledon in their next match by the narrow margin of 32-30, in spite of the continued absence of Lees and Whitfield.

After two more defeats (against West Ham and Sheffield) and a convincing 48-15 win over Plymouth, in which Watson, Kilmister and Van Praag all scored maximums, Wembley found themselves once more up against the all-conquering Belle Vue. It was the same old story. Even without Langton, the Aces thrashed the Lions by 42 points to 21 at the Empire Stadium. The baton of greatness had truly changed hands.

The final league table showed Wembley still in sixth place, the lowest placed of all the five London teams, with 39 points, while Belle Vue were by far and away the champions with 62 points, 16 points in front of runners-up Wimbledon.

The final match of the season at the Empire Stadium was a challenge match between Wembley and the English Test riders due to visit Australia over the winter. All supporters' club members from any club in the country were admitted at Wembley supporters' prices.

For a team that had won the treble just the season before, it had proved to be a disastrous campaign. True, they had managed to retain the London Cup and had reached the final of the National Trophy, but sixth place in the league and the nature of their defeat in that final showed they had a steep hill to climb to get back to being the major force in speedway. Injuries at various times to all their top riders – Lees, Watson, Van Praag and Kilmister had not helped and Elvin and Jackson could only hope that 1934 would bring better luck in terms of injuries and that a settled team would bring better results.

1933 National League Averages – qualification 6 matches

	Matches	Rides	Points	BP	Total	CMA
Wally Kilmister	33	98	222.5	6	228.5	9.33
Ginger Lees	23	69	147	8	155	8.99
Gordon Byers	35	103	174	23	197	7.65
Colin Watson	29	86	139.5	19	158.5	7.37
Harry Whitfield	24	63	98	12	110	6.98
Lionel Van Praag	33	94	126	24	150	6.38
Norman Evans	27	71	62	16	78	4.39
Reg Bounds	21	55	42	13	55	4.00
Hal Herbert	6	8	6	2	8	4.00

National League Matches

Date	H/A	Against	W/L/D	Score
4 May	Away	Coventry	Won	34-27
9 May	Away	West Ham	Lost	16.5-46.5
11 May	Home	Crystal Palace	Won	34-29
15 May	Away	Wimbledon	Won	38-25
18 May	Home	Belle Vue	Won	38-23
20 May	Away	Clapton	Lost	18-44
23 May	Away	Plymouth	Lost	29-34
25 May	Home	Wimbledon	Lost	25-37
1 June	Home	Nottingham	Won	45-16
3 June	Away	Belle Vue	Lost	30-32
5 June	Away	Nottingham	Won	35-24
8 June	Home	Coventry	Won	37-21
14 June	Away	Sheffield	Won	38-25
22 June	Home	West Ham	Won	38-24
24 June	Away	Crystal Palace	Lost	23-39
6 July	Home	Plymouth	Won	46-17
8 July	Away	Belle Vue	Lost	31-32
13 July	Home	Clapton	Won	49.5-13.5
20 July	Home	Sheffield	Won	37-26
7 August	Away	Coventry	Lost	21-42
10 August	Home	Clapton	Drew	31-31
12 August	Away	Clapton	Lost	28-34
23 August	Away	Nottingham	Won	37-25
7 September	Home	Wimbledon	Lost	24-38
7 September	Home	Coventry	Won	35-28
12 September	Away	Plymouth	Lost	27-35
16 September	Away	Crystal Palace	Lost	21-42
19 September	Away	West Ham	Lost	27-36
21 September	Home	Crystal Palace	Won	35-27
21 September	Home	Sheffield	Won	51-12
2 October	Away	Wimbledon	Won	32-30
4 October	Away	Sheffield	Lost	30-33
5 October	Home	West Ham	Lost	28-35
5 October	Home	Plymouth	Won	48-15
12 October	Home	Belle Vue	Lost	21-42
12 October	Home	Nottingham	Won	46-17

National League Table

	Played	Won	Drawn	Lost	For	Against	Points
Belle Vue	36	31	0	5	1,358.5	889.5	62
Wimbledon	36	23	0	13	1,213	1,027	46
West Ham	36	21	3	12	1,196.5	1,007.5	45
Crystal Palace	36	21	0	15	1,225	1,006	42
Clapton	36	19	3	14	1,204	1,036	41
WEMBLEY	36	19	1	16	1,184	1,057	39
Coventry	36	10	2	24	998	1,237	22
Sheffield	36	11	0	25	961	1,282	22
Plymouth	36	11	0	25	922	1,323	22
Nottingham	36	9	1	26	898	1,295	19

National Trophy

First Round
Wembley 103 Nottingham 22
Nottingham 44 Wembley 79
Aggregate: Wembley 182 Nottingham 66

Semi-Final
Wembley 77 Crystal Palace 48
Crystal Palace 62 Wembley 63
Aggregate: Wembley 140 Crystal Palace 110

Final
Wembley 54 Belle Vue 72
Belle Vue 92 Wembley 33
Aggregate: Belle Vue 164 Wembley 87

London Cup

First Round
Wembley: Bye

Semi-Final
Wembley 77 West Ham 46
West Ham 60 Wembley 66
Aggregate: Wembley 143 West Ham 106

Final
Wembley 69 Wimbledon 56
Wimbledon 53 Wembley 71
Aggregate: Wembley 140 Wimbledon 109

NO. 3 – HAROLD RILEY 'GINGER' LEES

Born in 1905 in Bury, Lancashire, Harry Riley Lees, known as 'Ginger' because of his thick shock of red hair, was one of the leading motorcyclists from the North of England before the advent of speedway. His first venture into competitive motorcycling was at the age of fourteen when he took part in road racing, trials, rough-riding events and grass track racing. In 1927 he won the Gold Medal in the International Six Days' Trial, one of motorcycling's premier events and, in 1928, he finished nineteenth in the Isle of Man Junior TT race, riding a New Imperial.

When Audenshaw staged the first recognised speedway meeting in Manchester on 3 March 1928, the spectators witnessed Lees, mounted on a Rudge-Whitworth, sweep the board. He moved on to Manchester White City and then, when league racing began in 1929, he signed up for Burnley. When tentative moves were made to introduce speedway to the Continent, Lees was among the pioneers, riding in both Denmark and Germany. In Germany in particular he was idolised and at the end of every meeting he found himself and his bike garlanded with flowers.

It is said that Lees originated the foot-forward style of riding. When the Australians and Americans brought the sport to this country they were all exponents of the spectacular leg-trailing style. Lees reasoned that if you didn't have to lean your bike so far over sideways entering a corner, as all the leg-trailers had to do, it would become upright much earlier leaving the bend and so give more tyre traction. Instead of trailing his left leg, therefore, he pushed it forward on entering the bends. He did this to such an exaggerated extent that, at times, it looked as though he was standing over his bike. But it worked and this style of riding was soon adopted by other top-class riders including Eric Langton, Joe Abbott, Gus Kuhn and Wembley's Harry Whitfield.

He moved to Liverpool in 1930 and Preston in 1931. By then, he had become one of the top English riders in the sport and was chosen to ride for his country in the third England *v.* Australia Test match of 1931 at Wembley. Although he had never seen the track before he won his first race and recorded the fastest time of the night, just three-fifths of a second outside the track record.

Lees' Test match debut did not go unnoticed by the Wembley management and he was soon signed up for the Lions by Johnnie Hoskins. He easily topped the Lions' averages in 1932 with a cma of 10.25. In 1933 he suffered from an ankle injury and his average dropped to 8.99,

Ginger Lees.

though when he was fit he still showed what he could do, scoring 54 points out of a possible 60 between 22 June and 13 July. He returned to the top of the Wembley averages the following year with 9.88 but the following year he broke his ankle in Wembley's first league match of the season. He made a brief comeback during the season and then retired, but was persuaded to make a comeback in 1936. Although his scoring power was down on his best years, he still maintained an 8.00 average as the Lions' third heat leader, a position he maintained in 1937, at the end of which he finally retired for good.

He was an automatic choice for England between 1931 and 1934 and at the end of 1934 he was England's all-time top scorer. He returned to ride for England in 1936 and 1937. At the end of his Test career he had ridden 21 times for England and scored 197 points. He still holds the record for the highest scores in individual Test matches, scoring 20 in the first Test of 1933 and 22 in the second Test. This was under the 4-2-1 scoring system.

Lees reached the final stages of the Star Championship in 1932 and again in 1934 when he finished third. He also reached two World Championship finals, finishing fourteenth in 1936 and ninth in 1937.

He was very confident and self-assured, almost to the point of cockiness, but he could deliver when challenged. One day at the Empire Pool he was swimming with some other Wembley riders when he boasted that he could do a swallow dive off the top diving board. The others dared him to try. Lees climbed up the tall ladder and made a dive an Olympic champion would have been proud of.

On his retirement he concentrated on his motor car business. In 1938, the Great Britain RAC Rally team prize was won by the three Rileys entered by Lees.

SEVEN

1934 – THE LIONS BOUND BACK... ALMOST

Before the start of the new season Wembley were able to announce a major new incentive to join the supporters' club. A new indoor arena and swimming pool, to be called the Empire Pool, was about to be added to the Wembley complex. Due to open in July 1934, members of the speedway supporters' club would be given special facilities for admission and when, in October, the new Wembley Lions Ice Hockey club commenced operations, speedway supporters' club members would automatically become members of the ice hockey supporters' club for no additional payment.

Already the largest supporters' club in the country, this new incentive encouraged even faster growth in club membership. Just before the speedway season started, the Wembley management were able to announce that the club had twice as many members as the previous year and that applications were being received at the rate of 800 a day.

During the previous season starting had still been causing problems. It was hoped that with the change from rolling starts to clutch starts and then the introduction of starting gates, jumping the start would be a thing of the past, but the riders had learnt to anticipate the tapes going up by watching the steward. A slight movement of the hand was enough for them to realise that he was about to release the gate. So, for the 1934 season a new rule was implemented that all tracks had to install electronically operated gates to be operated by the steward from a place where he could not be seen by the riders. Another rule change was the return to the 3-2-1 method of scoring.

Towards the end of March, Jackson announced his contracted riders for the forthcoming season as Watson (captain), Kilmister, Lees, Whitfield, Byers, Van Praag and Bounds from the 1933 team plus Greenwood, who had returned from Nottingham, Eric Gregory, and Jack Dixon, signed up from Belle Vue, and Australians Wally Little, Ken Kirkman and Jack Millward. Norman Evans, Maurice Stobart and Cliff Parkinson were released.

Nine teams had applied to take part in the National League. As well as Wembley, these were Belle Vue, Birmingham, Harringay, Lea Bridge, New Cross, Plymouth, West Ham and Wimbledon.

Although Watson was now the oldest rider still riding regularly in league speedway, his form was still good enough to justify his inclusion in the team as captain. In the Lions' first fixture of the season, a challenge match away at Wimbledon, he top scored for Wembley with 8 points,

A Wembley supporter's home-made postcard with the photographs and autographs of Wally Kilmister and Jack Dixon.

winning two races and being the only Lion to defeat the Dons' Vic Huxley and Claude Rye. Wembley lost the match 30-24.

It was not an auspicious start to a season that Wembley were desperate to do well in to show their critics that 1933 had been a one-off. Determined to return to the number one spot, Jackson decided that the key to their comeback was physical fitness, so he organised even more physical training sessions under trainer Ted Husbands.

The team got off to a flying start in the league as they beat Harringay away on 21 April in their first league match of the season. The 28-26 scoreline owed much to their three heat leaders as Kilmister dropped just one point, scoring 8, while Watson and Lees contributed 6 each. This was followed by another away win three days later, this time at West Ham, when once again Watson scored 8 points. This time it was Van Praag and Byers who provided the support, scoring 6 each. Although it was early in the season, it looked as though Wembley were definitely on their way back, with the whole team performing well. This was particularly true of the veteran Watson, who had now scored 24 points out of a possible 27 in his first three matches. As the first Test was due to be raced at Wembley, Jackson forwarded a strong claim to the selectors to name Watson as England captain.

Good as this start was, what was to come was even better as Wembley enjoyed the sweet taste of revenge by inflicting the first defeat of the season on their bitter rivals, Belle Vue, at Hyde Road. Watson's claim to captain England was strengthened even further as he went through the card undefeated, scoring maximum points and recording the two fastest times of the night. The Byers/Lees partnership scored 12 out of a possible 15 points between them, and that only because Byers was excluded in one heat. The final score was close, 26-28, but nevertheless it was an important away victory for the Lions.

This win gave the supporters' club a tremendous fillip – on the Monday following the meeting no fewer than 2,000 applications were received, while the next day a further 1,000 rolled in. The club secretary estimated that by the time of Wembley's opening on 10 May there were likely to be between 17,000 and 18,000 members.

Watson's stunning return to form continued in the next match, away at Plymouth, as he scored another maximum in his team's 30-25 win. Kilmister was also in top form, registering

8 points. The season had started with four away matches and four victories. The team that had set the Lions off in the manner to which they had formerly been accustomed was Watson/Greenwood; Byers/Lees; Kilmister/Van Praag.

The Empire Stadium opened its doors to speedway again on 10 May with a league match against Wimbledon. In effect, this turned into a duel between Huxley on the one hand and the whole of the Wembley team on the other. The opening heat saw a 5-1 to the Dons as Huxley and Pymar got the better of Watson and Greenwood. By heat three the Dons were 10-8 up but in the crucial heat four, Lees, riding at his superb best, got ahead of Huxley and stayed there for four laps. It was Huxley's only defeat of the night. In the end, it was a comfortable enough victory for the Lions as they ran out winners by 31 points to 23.

In the second half of the meeting, Watson equalled the Cinders record of 18.8 seconds, but Huxley went one better, beating it with a time of 18.6 seconds to become the new one-lap record holder and holder of the Cinders Trophy.

The opening night brought in yet more members for the supporters' club, including one group from Devon, who said they intended to travel up for every home meeting. Another member, a headmaster in Norwich, said he planned to bring twenty of his pupils to the match against Lea Bridge later in the year. As forecast, membership reached the 18,000 mark.

Still unbeaten, but with a slight change to the team as Whitfield came in to replace Greenwood, the Lions travelled next to New Cross, who had taken Crystal Palace's place in the league with more or less the same team. The match proved to be one of the most exciting of the season so far as, right from heat one, when Watson got the better of Stan Greatrex and Ron Johnson to record a 3-3, the match continued fairly evenly until the start of heat eight, by which time the Lambs (as New Cross were originally known), were one point behind. As heat eight started, their captain, Johnson, shot into an early lead and looked all set to win when he dropped a valve and wrecked his engine. This handed the Lions a 5-1 on a plate and an unassailable lead. Although the unbeaten Tom Farndon won the last heat for New Cross, it was too late and Wembley maintained their unbeaten run with a 29-24 victory. Kilmister top scored with 8 while Watson scored 7.

Wembley had no difficulty in overcoming their next opponents, West Ham, at home, but the match provided the most exciting race seen at the Empire Stadium for a long time between Byers and Tiger Stevenson in heat four. Byers gated first, gaining a small lead as the pair entered the first bend. On the back straight, the West Ham captain, lying flat on top of his bike, managed to gain a fractional lead by sheer speed, only to have it taken away by Byers' stupendous corner work. This procedure went on throughout the entire race as Stevenson led on the straights, only to have his lead taken away on the bends. Both men were riding superbly and absolutely cleanly, each holding his own line perfectly and there was not a hint of boring or cutting up at any point in the race. In the end, Stevenson's speed on the final straight just saw him take the chequered flag by inches. A loud cheer greeted the two riders as they shot over the line. The final match score was Wembley 35 West Ham 17. Kilmister contributed a maximum 9 points.

The next away match was against Wimbledon and it was very much a re-run of what had happened when the two teams met at the Empire Stadium, as it turned into a Huxley v. Wembley match. Huxley won his three heats but had no real support from his teammates as Wembley continued their unbeaten run with a 32-21 victory. Top scorers for Wembley were Watson with 8, Lees 7, Kilmister 6 and Byers 5.

Wembley's next home match was against bottom of the table Plymouth. The Lions seized the opportunity to show just what a powerful side they were by trouncing their opponents 40-14. Strangely though, Plymouth's one race win, by Frank Pearce, was in a new track record time of 78.2 seconds, beating the old mark of 78.4 seconds set by Belle Vue's Frank Charles. Lees and Watson were joint top scorers with 8 each.

Both Lees and Kilmister rode well in the London Riders' Championship, which was held at New Cross on 30 May. Lees reached the final, where he finished third behind two of the greatest riders of all time, Tom Farndon and Vic Huxley. Kilmister just failed to reach the final; although he had the same number of points as Huxley he lost out by virtue of the fact that when the two had met Huxley had beaten him.

There was a shock in store for the rampant Lions in their next match as they were defeated by Harringay at home to record their first loss of the season, the final score being Wembley 23 Harringay 31. Although Harringay were helped out by the fact that Kilmister suffered mechanical problems in two heats, they nevertheless deserved the win as the Parker brothers, Jack and Norman, were on top form, though they were both forced to lower their colours to Lees, who scored a maximum. The *Speedway News* felt, in an editorial specially devoted to Wembley's first defeat of the season, that they had become 'slightly slack' and that Harringay had pounced on this.

This defeat put Wembley equal with Belle Vue as both had now lost just one match. Coincidentally, Wembley's next tie was at home to the Aces, a match that now became crucial to the Lions' hopes of regaining the league title.

Before this took place, however, there was the little matter of the first Test at the Empire Stadium. Watson was duly appointed captain following his excellent early season form, but he only managed 6 points as England went down to a heavy 69-38 defeat. Lees was once again England's top scorer with 15 points. He won his first three races and was his team's only heat winner after the interval. He was partnered by his Wembley teammate Byers, who scored just 2 points. Van Praag represented Australia, scoring 6.5. The match was remarkable for the fact that Pearce's track record of 78.2 seconds was broken no less than five times, including three times by Lees, though it was Farndon who finished up with the new track record, knocking a whole second off to record 77.2 seconds in heat two. The other rider to beat the old record was Australia's Max Grosskreutz.

Just before the eagerly awaited clash with Belle Vue, Jackson announced that, although she lived in the village of Turriff, forty miles north of Aberdeen, his mother had joined the supporters' club, becoming the oldest member at seventy-three years of age. The membership figure now stood at 20,400, one of whom, member number 16,784, was the famous lawn tennis player and former Wimbledon champion Suzanne Lenglen.

Suddenly, after their wonderful start to the season, Wembley were back in trouble. Slow motors and a 'lack of spirit' were blamed for their home defeat at the hands of their great rivals and nearest competitors Belle Vue. The *Speedway News*, which had already referred to their slackness in the Harringay defeat, returned to the theme after the Belle Vue match, 'Slow motors are undoubtedly one of Wembley's chief troubles at the moment, but there is also a lack of spirit in the riding of some of the members of the team… Ginger Lees is the outstanding example of what a Lion should be but the Lions have recently degenerated into little more than a one-man team, though Lionel Van Praag is putting his back into it and improving every week.' Jackson was disgusted by what he saw as lack of effort on the part of most of his team. After the match he said, 'I'm going to have a new device fitted on most of the Wembley machines so that when the throttle is wide open it will ring a bell, but as soon as the throttle is closed it will blow a raspberry.'

It was true that Lees was the only rider who put up any sort of challenge to the Aces. He scored 7 points but even he was beaten by Langton, who scored a maximum, and Grosskreutz. Their clash in heat two was one of the greatest races seen at Wembley. Both men flew off from the start with Lees on the inside. For the whole four laps he remained on the white line, while Grosskreutz took the outside line. They passed and repassed so many times it was impossible to count. On the last bend of the last lap, Lees drifted off the white line and right out towards the fence, forcing Grosskreutz to go out with him. Grosskreutz, in a daring move, decided to leave his throttle wide open and, as they neared the fence he refused to be pushed any further, turning slightly back in towards Lees. His machine control was amazing and, on the run-in, he just edged past Lees, winning the race by mere inches.

The final score was Wembley 23 Belle Vue 31. Apart from the result and its significance, the talk of the evening was of the great show put up in the second half of the meeting by Wembley's young Australian junior, Wally Little. In his first season in England he won his heat and semi-final of the scratch race and found himself up against Langton, Huxley and Lees in the final, but the awesome company didn't seem to faze him as he kept calm to finish third, beating Huxley in the process. Little had just been named in Wembley's junior team as a new Second Division competition was announced made up of junior teams from Belle Vue, Birmingham, Harringay, New Cross, Wembley, West Ham and Wimbledon. He was joined in the Wembley junior team by Jack Millward and Ken Kirkman.

Following a good talking to by Jackson, more physical training and a thorough look at the team's motors at their own testing facility, the Lions bounced back in their next match, beating Birmingham at the latter's own track by 34 points to 20. The match also heralded a return to form for Watson, who came away with a maximum 9 points. Greenwood returned for the match and also showed a welcome return to form as he contributed 5 points. Van Praag scored a paid maximum.

Two days later, the Lions' renaissance continued as they demolished an understrength Lea Bridge team by 35 points to 17. It was a visiting rider, Dicky Case, however, who took the honours with a fine maximum.

Before the match, Wembley held their eliminating contest to find their two representatives for the Star Riders' Championship. The final came down to a contest between Lees, Van Praag and Watson. Lees led throughout with Van Praag chasing him well. On the third lap Watson ran round the outside of his Australian teammate to gain second place and that was how it finished, leaving Lees and Watson as Wembley's championship contenders.

Watson showed that his return to form was continuing when, on 26 June, he rode for England against a team labelled 'The Rest' in a Test trial. He top scored for England with 16 points. He was in such good form, in fact, that the *Speedway News* complained that 'Watson was usually so much better than anyone else that his races were not very interesting.' Four other Wembley riders took part in the meeting, Byers scoring 12 and Lees 8 for England while for 'The Rest' Kilmister totalled 10 and Van Praag 4.

When the end-of-June averages were released they confirmed just what a successful season Watson had been having, as he was in fifth place with a cma of 9.44. Lees was also having a good season. He was in seventh place with a cma of 8.72.

Next up for Wembley was the National Trophy first round first leg tie against Harringay. Raced on a very wet evening with several stoppages and steward inspections, the Lions managed to gain a ten-point advantage to take back to Green Lanes for the return leg. In spite of a poor track due to the incessant rain, Lees managed to end the evening with 17 points in Wembley's 59-49 victory. Van Praag, who only managed to score 3 points, suffered from engine trouble all night. In heat thirteen his magneto came adrift. He was so angry about it that when he got back to the pits he put a large dent into a bucket of water with his foot then threw a couple of wooden benches into the air, following this up by hurling a bag of fruit across the pits. As the riders around him scattered, Jackson calmly walked up to him and remarked, 'What's to do? Letting off a bit of steam?' Van Praag saw the funny side immediately and calmed down.

For the return at Harringay two days later, the riders found they had the opposite problem as the track proved to be very dry and slick. With ten points to pull back from the first leg, the Tigers got off to a good start as Jack Parker and Bill Dallison managed a 4-2 over Watson in heat one. But disaster struck them in heats two and six and after that they were never really in the match. In heat two neither of their riders, Norman Parker nor former Lion Norman Evans, finished. Evans was excluded for breaking the tapes and then Parker let in his clutch too suddenly as the gates rose and he reared and fell off his bike, aggravating an old back injury. For the rest of the meeting he was little more than a passenger.

But far worse was in store for Harringay in the sixth heat. Phil Bishop, who had won his first race, was fighting furiously for first place with Kilmister in heat five when his machine became entangled with the safety fence. Bishop came off his bike looking very much the worse for wear. However, he insisted on taking his next ride, which, as it turned out, was in the next heat, the fateful heat six. He was still feeling shaken from his previous heat fall and, for no apparent reason, he slid from his bike while the race was on. Bishop's partner, Charlie Blacklock, was unable to avoid him as he lay on the track, hitting him hard in the body. Blacklock himself was thrown over the handlebars but got to his feet quickly, unhurt. Bishop, however, was taken to hospital with what looked like serious injuries and took no further part in the match. To all intents and purposes, Harringay were now two heat leaders down and, after heat six, 5-1s for the Lions became the rule rather than the exception and they ran out 74-33 winners on the night, 133-82 on aggregate, although, because Jack Parker managed to put on a brave lone display, only Lees emerged with a maximum for Wembley.

Just after the Harringay match, Reg Bounds announced his retirement from the sport. He had never really recovered from his serious crash at Lea Bridge and, although he had made a comeback the previous season, he had never regained anything like his old form. In the end he reluctantly decided that he should retire and devote his time to his garage in Kilburn. It was a sad end for a promising rider.

Returning to league racing on 4 July, the Lions found themselves on the wrong end of a narrow defeat at New Cross as they went down 28-26. Once again, Lees was top scorer for Wembley, his only defeat coming at the hands of the Lambs' captain and maximum man Ron Johnson. With three defeats to Belle Vue's two, Wembley now had some lost ground to make up in the second half of the season.

As part of his commitment to improve the machines of the Wembley riders so that they could put in a proper challenge to Belle Vue, Jackson had designed a new clutch that Kilmister had been trying out under match conditions. Jackson and Kilmister's opinion was that it was twice as easy to operate as a normal clutch and 'much sweeter' in action. Jackson decided that all the Wembley riders should switch to this equipment. In addition to his new clutch, Jackson was also concentrating on his policy of bringing on young riders and opened a training track at Luton Greyhound Stadium.

Wembley returned to winning ways in their next match, at home to Birmingham, with a 35-19 scoreline and another maximum from Lees as well as one from Byers. The second half of the match was a Second Division match between Wembley and Belle Vue. It resulted in a convincing victory for the Cubs by 23 points to 11. Little scored a paid maximum. Jackson was very pleased with his youngsters and could only hope that a similar scoreline would be the outcome of the forthcoming First Division match between the two teams.

In the meantime, the senior team had an away fixture at West Ham to fulfil, one that they won. With two heats to go, the scores were level at 21-21. Two 5-1s for the Lions, however, ensured a substantial enough 31-23 winning margin.

Wembley's next match was against Wimbledon in the London Cup first round first leg. Byers was once again in good form and contributed 14 points to the Lions' 60-47 victory. The second leg at Plough Lane also resulted in a Lions win as they defeated the Dons 57-48 to go through to the final, 117-95 on aggregate. It was a good all-round team effort as Kilmister, Lees and Van Praag all scored 12 and Byers 11 paid 12.

It was just as well that Byers was now coming into the best form of his life as it had become apparent that his riding partner and captain, Watson, was not the rider he had been at the start of the season. He seemed to be starting matches well but tiring as the night went on. He was no longer contributing high scores in the way he had been and was now giving Jackson some cause for concern. If Wembley were to snatch the title back from Manchester's finest, he needed his captain back to his old form, and quickly.

Two league wins in two days saw Wembley keep up the pressure as they disposed of New Cross 33-20 at home and Lea Bridge 31-23 away, Lees scoring a maximum in each match.

Another short break from league racing saw Wembley defeat New Cross yet again, this time in the first leg of the National Trophy semi-final. Lees kept up his breathtaking form, losing just twice to Johnson and recording 16 points. His first defeat at the hands of Johnson saw his opponent smash not only the New Cross clutch-start record but also the rolling-start record. This match also saw the return, after many months, of the famous Whitfield/Greenwood pairing and they rode together as though they'd never been split up. Whitfield's return to the team was occasioned by Kilmister's absence through tonsillitis. Watson was again down on scoring power, managing just 2 points. Nevertheless, it was a handsome 62-42 victory for the Lions, giving them a 20-point lead to take back to the Empire Stadium.

As expected, the second leg of the National Trophy semi-final was very one-sided as Wembley ran out victors by 67.5 to 40.5, taking the tie on aggregate 129.5 to 82.5. Lees led the way with an 18-point maximum. Greenwood, relishing the opportunity of riding with his old partner Whitfield, recorded his best score of the season with 15.

When the end-of-July averages came out, Watson's fall was obvious. He had dropped to eighth place in the averages, with a new average of 8.52. Not surprisingly, Lees was now Wembley's top rider, in sixth place with 9.41.

The end-of-July National League table showed that there were now only two teams in the hunt for honours. Belle Vue were still top with 36 points from 20 matches, having lost just two, while Wembley had 30 points from 18 matches, having lost three. Well behind them, in third place, were New Cross, who had lost eight matches and had 24 points from 20 matches.

With the team now going so well, Jackson agreed to release some of his juniors to help out other teams who were suffering from injuries. Gregory and Dixon moved over to West Ham, while Little was given the daunting task of replacing the injured Vic Huxley at Wimbledon.

Having dispersed the main elements of his Second Division team, Jackson then found himself in the difficult position of being a rider short for the match against Birmingham. There was only one thing to do and he did it. Jackson donned leathers and turned out for his own team. In his first and, as it turned out, only race, he shot away from the gate in first place and rounded the first bend in the lead. At that point he saw the fence approaching rather rapidly. He immediately slowed down, allowing the other three riders to sweep past him. It was enough for Jackson and his comeback was over.

Wembley were now in the National Trophy final and the semi-final of the London Cup, and were also still pushing for league honours. The treble was within their reach. There was also a fourth cup to be fought for this year as a new competition was introduced, the ACU Cup. This was, in speedway terms, a radical new departure as it was based on football's FA Cup, i.e. it would not be run on a home and away basis; there would be just one match deciding the tie. First out of the hat got the home draw.

With the opening of the new Empire Pool, Van Praag managed to find himself a new job as a swimming instructor and lifeguard. Back home in his native Australia he had won a number of important swimming events and was a brilliant swimmer. This move did wonders for the attendance at the pool as hundreds of Lions supporters decided they would now like to learn to swim.

Wembley continued their winning ways in their next home match against Lea Bridge. With Kilmister back, Jackson reshuffled his pairings, which now stood as Lees and Watson, Kilmister and Greenwood and Van Praag and Byers. Inevitably, Lees scored a maximum to help his team to a 32-21 win. Van Praag, obviously benefiting from his swimming exercise, also scored a maximum, while Greenwood dropped just one point to Dicky Case.

Two days later another victory came, this time away at Harringay, 32-22. Kilmister had returned to full fitness and returned the full 9 points. Kilmister added another maximum in the next match, an away victory at Wimbledon, as did Lees. Apart from Watson, who was still not showing his real form, the team had hit a purple patch and were all scoring well. They showed no mercy to a hapless Plymouth. Both Lees and Kilmister recorded full maximums, while Byers recorded a paid maximum in Wmbley's 41-12 demolition of the Devils. This was Lees' fourth home maximum on the trot and his splendid form was recognised by the board of control as they nominated him to meet Ron Johnson in an eliminator for the right to challenge Tom Farndon for his British Individual Championship. However, Lees declined the offer, letting it be known that he did not wish to be considered.

On 14 August Wembley had the honour of taking part in the first-ever ACU Cup match away at Birmingham. They were not fazed by this new competition or by having to ride the one and only leg away as they defeated the Brummies 59-49. Former Lion Jack Ormston was top scorer for Birmingham, but he could not match the firepower of Wembley alone as four riders, Lees, Van Praag, Greenwood and Kilmister, all went into double figures.

Watson showed something like his old form as the rampaging Lions added yet another scalp to their tally, beating West Ham 36-18. Lees and Watson scored 13 out of a possible 15 as a pair.

Wembley supporters were hoping that Watson was regaining his form at just the right time as the next meeting to be held at the Empire Stadium was the Star Riders' Championship final. Watson was one of Wembley's representatives, along with Lees. In his first outing in heat two it looked as though he was going to give his supporters something to cheer about as he electrified the crowd by chasing Bluey Wilkinson, catching him on the second lap and going into a two-lengths lead. Unfortunately his engine then seized up and he was out of the meeting; it was left to the Lions' form man, Lees, to carry the hopes of the fans. Out in the next heat, he had an easy win as Claude Rye fell while lying in second place. Lees was out again in the second semi-final against the New Cross pair Ron Johnson and George Newton. Lees and Johnson both got good starts and went round the first bend dead level, but as they straightened up Lees drew ahead and was very slightly faster on the straight. Two laps later, Johnson drew level again, but once more Lees went ahead. Glued to the white line all the way round he rode the race of his life to defeat Johnson in the fastest semi-final of the three.

Lees had now reached the final, the first time a Wembley rider had achieved this feat in the Star Championship. Unfortunately, he never really showed in the final, which became a race between Eric Langton and Jack Parker, with Parker just getting the better of the former. Nevertheless, third place was the highest position ever reached by a Wembley rider in the Star Championship and it made a 1-2-3 clean sweep for England. Lees received £25 for his third place. With his success in team racing, both for Wembley and England, and now his success as an individual rider, Lees had reached the very pinnacle of his career and was recognised throughout the speedway world as one of the greatest contemporary riders, putting him on a par with riders such as Parker, Langton, Huxley and Farndon. It was no mean feat.

The moment all Wembley supporters had been waiting for arrived the following Saturday, 25 August. It was the match against Belle Vue. If Belle Vue won, Wembley's chance of the league title would be virtually finished, but if Wembley could manage to pull off the victory the league title was theirs for the taking.

The supporters' club laid on a special excursion train leaving Euston at 12.10 p.m. and costing 10s return. The club secretary, Mr A.J. Bray, urged as many supporters as possible to go and support the team because 'your vocal support always acts as a great tonic to the Lions at away matches'.

The match started well for Wembley. The first heat was a 3-3 and then, in the second, Grosskreutz's machine packed up, leaving Van Praag and Byers to take a 5-1 over Kitchen. Heat three was another 3-3, leaving Wembley four points up going into heat four. But then it all went wrong as Grosskreutz and Kitchen managed a 5-1 over Lees, to be followed in the next heat by another 5-1 to Frank Charles and Joe Abbott. Not to be outdone, the Aces' third pairing, Langton and Varey, added one more in heat six. Heats seven and eight went the same way. Kilmister and Greenwood managed to stop the rot in heat nine, following Grosskreutz over the line for second and third places but by then the damage had been done. Wembley had lost the match by the massive margin of sixteen points, 35-19, and very probably the league title. Both the Lions' riders and fans were bitterly disappointed, not just because they had lost but by the nature of the loss. None of the team seemed to ride to their full capability in such a crucial fixture, the prime example being Lees, who managed just 4 points. Top scorer for Wembley was Kilmister with 5. After a month or so when they had seemed unstoppable, they had been stopped.

Les Bowden.

Although the Lions bounced back to win their next match, the London Cup semi-final first leg against West Ham, it was not a convincing victory as they managed to beat the Hammers by just six points on their own track. Lees was almost back at his best, scoring 16 points, losing out twice to Wilkinson, who scored a maximum for the visitors. Byers also rode well for the Lions, with 11 points. But a six-point winning margin was far less than the team had hoped for from a home match and it gave great heart to West Ham, who now thought they could overcome Wembley back at Custom House.

However, before they could race the return leg, the Lions had to return to Belle Vue on 1 September for the first leg of the National Trophy final. After the events of the previous week no-one gave them a hope. And they were right. Once again the Aces hammered Wembley, this time by 71 points to 36, to take a 35-point lead down to London.

The next week was to be a big week for the Lions, with the second legs of both cup matches, but first there was a small interlude as they took on Birmingham in the league. Although this was not seen as a very important fixture, given the two that were to follow, Jackson knew just how important it was for his team to win and get some of their confidence back. As it turned out, the match did prove to be important, though not for the right reason. Wembley duly won the match by 32 points to 22 with Lees back to maximum form but, in the very last heat of the match, Greenwood fell and broke his arm, putting him out for the rest of the season. His place in the Wembley team for the second leg of the London Cup semi-final was taken by Whitfield.

It was a large crowd, almost of Test match proportions, that assembled at Custom House on 11 September to witness the second leg. Wembley held a slender lead of six points but the writing was on the wall in the very first heat as Wilkinson shot off from Lees, winning by a distance in a new track record. His partner Gregory came third, beating Watson, and that was already two points pulled back. Wembley never really recovered and, in spite of some good riding by Lees (12 points) and Kilmister (11), they never really had a chance of stopping West

Ham gaining the six points and more they needed. In the end the Hammers won by 16 points, 62-46, putting an end once and for all to Wembley's dreams of the treble.

With Watson's form steadily getting worse and worse he decided that it was time to take a rest and withdrew from the team for the rest of the season. Whitfield also decided to retire. Lees was handed the captaincy and it was a new-look side that Jackson initially announced as his team for the National Trophy final second leg. Lees, Byers, Van Praag and Kilmister remained but into the team came two of the reserve team, Les Bowden and Jim Millward, with Ken Kirkman named as reserve. It was not a good time to have to make such wholesale changes and 'blood' the youngsters. Eventually, Jackson was able to persuade Watson and Whitfield to stay on. Because of the importance of the next few matches, they agreed.

There were those who thought that the Belle Vue team might not bother too much in the return leg and just be content to hang onto their big lead. That they did bother is self-evident from the final score, which was Wembley 34 Belle Vue 74. Langton scored a maximum and Grosskreutz and Abbott paid maximums. This on Wembley's own track.

Annoyingly for them, Wembley were drawn away at Belle Vue in the second round of the ACU Cup and unfortunately it was the same old tale as the Aces once again routed the Lions, this time by 79 points to 29.

Belle Vue were in a different class to Wembley and it was obvious it was going to take a lot of work in the close season to get the Lions in a position where they might challenge the Manchester team next year. Although they had lost the London Cup, the ACU Cup and the National Trophy, technically Wembley could still win the league and in their following two matches they defeated New Cross 28-25 and Plymouth away 32-22 to give themselves some faint hope. But their hopes of winning depended on the result of their home match against the Aces, which was still to come. Given the results of the previous meetings between the two, in both cup and league, it seemed a hopeless cause.

But even before that meeting took place, Wembley suffered a severe reverse in their campaign, losing at home to Harringay. It was the second time they had lost at home to Harringay in the league that season as it was the Tigers who had inflicted the first home defeat of the season on them back in May. The main reason for the loss was the lack of points from the man who had done so much to put Wembley in a position to challenge for the league title, Ginger Lees. He came second in his first race to Jack Parker but then, in his second, he collided with Phil Bishop and fell, scoring nothing. In his last heat he looked completely out of sorts, probably as a result of the fall, and trailed in a poor last. A total of 2 points from Lees is not what Wembley expected and was probably the reason they lost. Apart from that match he had scored 126 points in home league matches out of a possible 135.

The final confrontation with the Aces came on 27 September. This time it was Grosskreutz who did for the Lions, scoring 9 points and helping Belle Vue to yet another win, this time by 31 points to 23. Although Wembley won their last two matches, against Walthamstow (who had taken over from Lea Bridge) and Wimbledon, it was all over.

Frustratingly for Wembley, Belle Vue surprisingly slipped up twice in their last six matches, going down to Plymouth and West Ham and, in the end, Wembley only lost out on the title by two points. If only they hadn't lost to Harringay at home – twice… If only Lees hadn't collided with Bishop… if only Greenwood hadn't broken his arm… It was a season of 'if onlys' for Wembley.

THE EMPIRE STADIUM, WEMBLEY

MAGAZINE
PROGRAMME
PRICE

6ᴰ

WEMBLEY SPEEDWAY

THE "ASCOT" OF THE SPEEDWAYS

THURSDAY OCT. 11ᵀᴴ 1934 AT 8 P.M.

The programme cover from the meeting held on 11 October 1934. At this meeting Tom Farndon beat Max Grosskreutz 2-1 in the deciding leg of the British Match Race Championship. The old rolling start track record was beaten in all three races.

In the end-of-season averages, Lees finished in fifth place, behind Huxley, Langton, Parker and Farndon, with a cma of 9.88. Kilmister was the next Wembley rider, with a cma of 8.63, finishing in eleventh place. After his magnificent start to the season, Watson had dropped right down to twentieth place with an average of 7.73.

Jackson knew that he needed a new heat leader for 1935.

1934 National League Averages – qualification 6 matches

	Matches	Rides	Points	BP	Total	CMA
Ginger Lees	32	96	228	9	237	9.88
Wally Kilmister	32	95	192	13	205	8.63
Colin Watson	31	88	150	20	170	7.73
Lionel Van Praag	29	83	132	18	150	7.23
Gordon Byers	32	94	144	25	169	7.19
Harry Whitfield	16	44	56	17	73	6.64
George Greenwood	19	48	60	9	69	5.75
Wally Little	13	35	31	9	40	4.57
Les Bowden	7	20	14	3	17	3.40

National League Matches

Date	H/A	Against	W/L/D	Score
21 April	Away	Harringay	Won	28-26
24 April	Away	West Ham	Won	30-24
5 May	Away	Belle Vue	Won	28-26
8 May	Away	Plymouth	Won	30-23
10 May	Home	Wimbledon	Won	31-23
16 May	Away	New Cross	Won	29-24
17 May	Home	West Ham	Won	35-17
21 May	Away	Wimbledon	Won	32-21
24 May	Home	Plymouth	Won	40-14
31 May	Home	Harringay	Lost	23-31
14 June	Home	Belle Vue	Lost	23-31
19 June	Away	Lea Bridge	Won	35-17
4 July	Away	New Cross	Lost	26-28
5 July	Home	Birmingham	Won	35-19
10 July	Away	West Ham	Won	31-23
19 July	Home	New Cross	Won	33-20
20 July	Away	Lea Bridge	Won	31-23
2 August	Home	Lea Bridge	Won	32-21
4 August	Away	Harringay	Won	32-22
6 August	Away	Wimbledon	Won	32-20
9 August	Home	Plymouth	Won	41-12

16 August	Home	West Ham	Won	36-18
25 August	Away	Belle Vue	Lost	19-35
4 September	Away	Birmingham	Won	32-22
13 September	Home	Birmingham	Won	36-17
20 September	Home	New Cross	Won	28-25
25 September	Away	Plymouth	Won	32-22
27 September	Home	Belle Vue	Lost	23-31
3 October	Away	Walthamstow	Won	32-22
11 October	Home	Wimbledon	Won	29-24

National League Table

	Played	Won	Drawn	Lost	For	Against	Points
Belle Vue	32	27	0	5	1,040	650	54
WEMBLEY	32	26	0	6	980	731	52
New Cross	32	21	0	11	935.5	762.5	42
West Ham	32	16	1	15	865	841	33
Wimbledon	32	16	0	16	840	863	32
Harringay	32	14	1	17	867.5	837.5	29
Birmingham	32	9	0	23	757	949	18
Plymouth	32	8	2	22	668	1,007	18
Lea Bridge/Walthamstow	32	5	0	27	694	1,006	10

National Trophy

First Round
Wembley: Bye

Second Round
Wembley 59 Harringay 49
Harringay 33 Wembley 74
Aggregate: Wembley 133 Harringay 82

Semi-Final
Wembley 67.5 New Cross 40.5
New Cross 42 Wembley 62
Aggregate: Wembley 129.5 New Cross 82.5

Final
Belle Vue 71 Wembley 36
Wembley 34 Belle Vue 74
Aggregate: Belle Vue 145 Wembley 70

ACU Cup

First Round
Birmingham 49 Wembley 59

Second Round
Belle Vue 79 Wembley 29

London Cup

First Round
Wembley 60 Wimbledon 47
Wimbledon 48 Wembley 57
Aggregate: Wembley 117 Wimbledon 95

Semi-Final
West Ham 62 Wembley 46
Wembley 57 West Ham 51
Aggregate: West Ham 113 Wembley 103

Reserve League Results

Home Matches
Wembley 23 Belle Vue 11
Wembley 22 Birmingham 13
Wembley 18 Harringay 18
Wembley 19 New Cross 17
Wembley 8 West Ham 28
Wembley 22 Wimbledon 12

Away Matches
Belle Vue 7 Wembley 26
Birmingham 21 Wembley 13
Harringay 15 Wembley 18
New Cross 7 Wembley 28
West Ham 18 Wembley 18
Wimbledon 22 Wembley 13

Reserve League Table

	Played	Won	Drawn	Lost	For	Against	Points
West Ham	12	11	1	0	271	149	23
WEMBLEY	12	7	2	3	228	189	16
Harringay	12	6	1	5	218	200	13
Wimbledon	12	6	1	5	208	212	13
Birmingham	12	4	0	8	196	221	8
Belle Vue	12	3	0	9	174	241	6
New Cross	12	2	1	9	166	249	5

EIGHT

1935 – INJURIES AND A STAR

The 1935 season started with an announcement from the Wembley management that they had signed up one of the biggest stars in the history of the sport, none other than 'Cyclone' Billy Lamont. After a year's absence from racing in Great Britain, he was due to return on 17 April and take his place in the Wembley line-up. Another new name for the coming season was the Australian Dicky Smythe, who had last ridden in England in 1932 for Stamford Bridge. Dixon and Gregory also returned from spells at West Ham. The Lions' initial line-up was announced as Lees and Watson; Byers and Van Praag; Kilmister and Dixon with Gregory, Smythe and another newcomer, Ray Taylor, as reserves. Jackson was – wisely, as it turned out – waiting for Lamont to put in an appearance before actually assigning him a place in the team. Whitfield had finally retired and Greenwood was still not fully fit following his injury at the end of the previous season.

The league was composed of seven teams. Six were from London: Hackney Wick, Harringay, New Cross, Wembley, West Ham and Wimbledon. Then there were the champions, Belle Vue.

The first appearance of a Wembley team was in a Best Pairs competition at West Ham on 23 April and it was a complete disaster. The Lions were represented by Watson and Kilmister. All was going well until heat eight. It was in that heat that Watson's trailing leg hit a bump, jumped from the track and hit the chain on his bike with such tremendous force that the bone snapped in two places. Somehow, he managed to keep upright until he came to the finishing line. He then asked one of the starting officials to help him off his machine. His great presence of mind to stay on his bike probably saved him from even worse damage for, if he had fallen or tried to dismount on his own, the consequences might have been far worse. Many felt this could be Watson's last ever race as it was the third time he had broken the same leg. There was no doubting that he would be out for the season.

As if that wasn't bad enough, things were about to get worse. Wembley's first appearance as a full team took place a week later, again at West Ham. That the Lions lost the match 40-31 was the least of their problems. Having already lost Watson at Custom House, they now lost Lees, who took a nasty tumble straight into the safety fence. The prognosis was that he would be out for several weeks, but there was real concern in the Wembley camp that he might decide to call it a day permanently. Lees was the owner of a flourishing garage business in Bury and had for some time been muttering to his friends that he might give up speedway to concentrate on his business; now that he was sidelined through injury it was felt that he might take this opportunity to retire permanently.

Jackson had to move fast if Wembley were to retain any hope of putting in a realistic challenge for the season's honours. The date 17 April had come and gone and Lamont had still not arrived, so he decided he had to sign up another big name. His target was the Belle Vue star Frank Charles. Having driven 300 miles to visit Charles at his home in Barrow-in-Furness, he found him in bed with flu. Not wishing to disturb him too much he told him why he had come and drove the 300 miles back home again. The following day he received a telegram from Charles saying, 'Alec. Will ride for Wembley when fit. Perhaps two weeks. Frank.' Jackson then arranged the necessary transfer with Belle Vue. The arrangement he came to was that Charles would ride for Wembley in 1935. If they wished to retain him for 1936 they would then pay a transfer fee based on his performance during the year. It was thought that this fee was likely to be the highest in the history of the sport up to that point, somewhere into four figures.

With Charles signed up and Lamont now confirmed as being on his way at last, Jackson relaxed a little and summed up his team's prospects for 1935 as 'good'. In a quick rundown of the team, he had the following to say about each of the riders:

Lionel Van Praag, who had now assumed the captaincy in Lees' absence: 'We know how good he is, and he is determined to do even better to justify the confidence I have placed in him.'

Wally Kilmister: 'He is as good as ever.'

Gordon Byers and Bronco Dixon: 'They will ride as partners and will put the wind up the opposition, for you know them, "do or die".'

Dicky Smythe: 'He has proved his worth for, in a few rides, he has beaten some of the best. He was leading Dick Case at Belle Vue [in a second-half scratch race] when his tyre burst.'

Eric Gregory: 'He will support Wally and when he gets settled down he will be a hard man to beat.'

Billy Lamont: 'He arrives on 17 May and if he can reproduce his form of the Case–Lamont partnership, we shall have one of the best teams in the league.'

Ray Taylor: 'He has improved beyond all recognition.'

Jackson finished his rundown of the team on a very upbeat note, 'The Lions will roar louder than ever, and we shall be at the top of the table.'

While Jackson was in Barrow visiting Charles, he left his new captain, Van Praag, in charge of team practice. On his return, the other riders berated Jackson and told him that Van Praag was a 'rotten' boss as he made them ride until they were ready to drop and then shouted for more.

Wembley's opening fixture was against Wimbledon on 9 May. The racing format had been changed to twelve heats, but still with six rider teams and one reserve. Wembley's team for their opening home fixture was Van Praag/Smythe, Kilmister/Gregory, Byers/Dixon with Bowden as reserve. The Lions started well with two 4-2s and were therefore 8-4 up after heat two. Wimbledon fought back with two 4-2s of their own and from then on the match progressed fairly evenly until, with one heat to go, the score stood at Wembley 32 Wimbledon 33. There was a tense expectation from the crowd as their two top riders, Van Praag and Kilmister, came out to face Huxley and Geoff Pymar. But if they were expecting a hell-for-leather, no-holds-barred sort of race they were to be disappointed as Huxley flew off from the start and never looked like being caught. With Van Praag and Kilmister filling second and third places, the match score was Wembley 35 Wimbledon 36. Not the sort of start to his league campaign Jackson was looking for. The most positive points he could take from the meeting was the form of Kilmister and Van Praag, who scored 10 and 9 respectively. Smythe seemed to spend the evening looking after other riders' interests. In heat six he laid down his bike to avoid the fallen Wimbledon rider Jack Sharp, and then in heat eight he did the same to avoid another Wimbledon rider Wal Phillips, only this time he badly injured his finger.

With Charles and Lamont still not available to replace Watson and Lees, the Lions had the daunting task of visiting Belle Vue for their next match. Van Praag was Wembley's only race winner, in heat four, and that was only because Abbott's engine burst, littering parts all over the track. The end result was a 46-25 massacre for the Aces against the makeshift Lions.

With the imminent arrival of Charles, Jackson hoped that things would soon look up, but before he could put in an appearance, Hackney Wick complained that Charles should have gone to them as they were a much weaker team than Wembley. Although the control board dismissed the complaint, the fact is that Charles would not have gone there anyway. He had always made little secret of the fact that his ambition was to ride for Wembley and would have rather retired than go to Hackney.

Things at last started to look up for the Lions as they won their next match by ten points, 41-31, over Harringay. Charles made his debut for the home side and rode well for his 5 points, especially as a broken chain put him out of one heat. Once again, though, it was Van Praag and Kilmister who starred for Wembley, each scoring 9 points. But there were more problems for the Lions as, in the last heat, Kilmister clashed with former Lion Jack Ormston and, although it was Ormston who fell and Kilmister who finished, it was Kilmister who injured his foot and looked doubtful for the following evening's away fixture.

Ironically, that away fixture was at Hackney, who, with Kilmister missing from the Lions' line-up, showed no signs of being 'weaker' than Wembley as they defeated them with some ease, by 43 points to 28. Charles won his opening ride but he quickly tired and did not score another point all night. In the absence of Kilmister, it was left to Van Praag to bear the brunt of the scoring, totalling 9 points. Gregory also rode well for his 7.

When the league table was published on 22 May, it showed Wembley at the bottom of the league with just 2 points from 5 matches, while at the top of the league Belle Vue were unbeaten in 7.

Wembley were now without the services of Watson, Lees, Kilmister and Smythe. Injuries had decimated the Lions and moving up from their unaccustomed place in the league's cellar position looked almost impossible.

Wembley's next home match was against West Ham on 23 May. Great hopes were pinned on Lamont, who had at last arrived, ready to take his place in the team. And with Kilmister declaring himself fit, the fans had great hopes of the Wembley revival starting.

But it was not to be. Kilmister rode in just two races, scoring 1 point, before pulling out again and as for Lamont, his antics finished off any chance Wembley had of returning to winning ways. As he came out onto the track he was given one of the greatest receptions accorded to any rider in the history of the Empire Stadium. Even those who had never seen him ride cheered like mad at just the mention of his name. His reputation wenr before him and he wasn't long in proving that the stories of his recklessness were well-earned. Dubbed 'the man with a month to live' because of the way he rode, Lamont was soon providing his usual fireworks.

'Cyclone' Billy Lamont, 'the man with a month to live'.

As the tapes went up for his first race, it was his teammate Dixon who took the lead, sticking close to the white line. Lamont was half a length behind, right on the outside fence, hurtling along like an express train, depositing most of the cinders onto the dog track. Close on their tails was West Ham's Tiger Stevenson, looking for an opening to break up the 5-1 the Lions now held in their grasp. Then came the tragedy. Dixon swerved out just as Lamont swerved in and the two machines came together and turned turtle. Both riders went sprawling while Stevenson, still close behind, dived straight into the wreckage. It was the end of Lamont's evening and with both him and Kilmister now out, the Lions had no chance, finally losing 42-28. Dixon recovered from the crash and went on to end the evening as Wembley's top scorer with 9 points, but it was not an auspicious start from Lamont and it was touch and go whether he too would be added to the ever-growing injury list after just one match.

Fortunately, Lamont was not too badly injured and he took his place in the Wembley side for their next match against Belle Vue. With Watson, Lees and Kilmister still missing, Jackson managed to talk Harry Whitfield into returning to the saddle for his old team. Nevertheless, it was still very much a 'B' team that now took on the might of the champions and the only unbeaten team in the league. No-one gave them much chance.

But the team pulled together magnificently and Van Praag proved to be an inspirational captain, taking the fight to the Aces. With one heat to go, Wembley held a slender one-point lead, but with the Belle Vue captain Eric Langton and Bill Kitchen out in the last heat, the Lions, in the shape of Van Praag and Charles, looked to have their work cut out to hold on and win the match for Wembley. As the tapes went up it was the two Lions who got away first, but Langton chased hard after them and soon passed Charles, The crowd grew frantic with excitement as he closed the gap between himself and Van Praag, but the Lions' captain just held on to win at the line by inches to a storm of applause that was heard all over Wembley town. With that 4-2 in the final heat, Wembley turned out to be the surprise 37-34 winners and inflicted Belle Vue's first defeat of the season. All the team rode well. Van Praag top scored with 10 while Dixon added 7 in just three rides. Even Whitfield made a solid contribution in his first match back, with 5 points.

Unfortunately the winning streak was confined to one match as two days later the Lions found themselves on the wrong end of a 41-30 scoreline at Harringay. But the good news for Wembley was that, for the first time, Charles showed his true class, scoring 11 points, losing just once to the Harringay captain, Jack Parker.

Even without their three main stars from the start of the season, Watson, Lees and Kilmister, the Wembley team was now beginning to gel. Van Praag was riding better than ever and Charles was at last coming back to form. Behind them, Dixon had made a great start to the season and was rapidly becoming a recognised third heat leader. The only disappointment was the form of Lamont, who just could not regain the form he had shown earlier in his career.

For the next match, away at Wimbledon, it all came together again as Van Praag scored 10, Charles 9, Dixon 8 and Byers 7 to record a great 41-29 victory over the Dons. Once again though, Lamont scored 0.

The Empire Stadium's next meeting was the first Test match of the season, won by England by 56 points to 52. Two Wembley riders were chosen, Charles for England, scoring 11, and Van Praag for Australia, scoring 8.

The format of the ACU Cup was changed for 1935. Instead of being run on a straight one-match knock-out basis it was run on a pool system. Belle Vue, Wimbledon and Wembley formed one pool, while the other four formed the second. Each team met each of the others in their pool home and away and the team with the highest aggregate race points score from each pool would meet in the final.

Wembley's first ACU Cup match was away at Belle Vue. It was a very boring match as, apart from former Ace Charles, the rest of the team put up no fight at all, even though Kilmister had returned. Charles was Wembley's only winner, coming first in three heats. The final score was Belle Vue 74 Wembley 32.

Wembley soon bounced back after this bad defeat and won their next two matches, beating New Cross away 38-34 in the league, Charles scoring 10 and Kilmister 9, and Wimbledon 72-35 at home in the ACU Cup, with Kilmister right back to form scoring an 18-point maximum and Charles scoring 16.

Lamont had missed these matches as he felt he was not match fit. Under the guidance of Ted Husbands he embarked on a rigorous get-fit course. At one session, after doing a spot of ball punching in the gym, he decided to take a bath and have a good rub down, after which he was standing around naked, feeling like taking a few minutes to rest, so he sat down. Unfortunately he sat down on the hot-water pipes, with the result that he had to have plaster stuck on a place that made it very difficult to sit down and ride a speedway bike for a while!

Two more points came Wembley's way in their next home match against Hackney as the three heat leaders were now fully in their stride, Charles scoring a paid maximum, Van Praag 11 and Kilmister 10. The final score was Wembley 42 Hackney 28.

Wembley's run of victories came to an abrupt halt at Belle Vue the following Saturday as, for the third time that season, the Aces proved too strong for them. With his local track knowledge, Charles was once again the Lions' only heat winner as they suffered a 49-23 reverse.

Far left: Eric Gregory.

Left: Frank Charles in full flight. (John Chaplin collection)

Back home the following week, Wembley were on much safer territory as, on the night, they beat New Cross 39-33. However, New Cross protested at the result and it was changed to 38-34. The whole match suffered from poor stewarding. The first incident occurred in heat three when Gregory caught Farndon and both went down with a crash. Whether accidental or not, the collision was definitely Gregory's fault and he should have been excluded. Even the Wembley supporters were surprised when no exclusion light came on. Seeing that he wasn't excluded, Gregory quickly remounted, rode across the grass, turned round and came back on to the track where he had left it and finished the race to be awarded 1 point for finishing third. The tables were turned in heat seven when Gregory himself was knocked off by Johnson. Johnson miraculously kept upright while he negotiated the obstacle of Gregory's fallen bike. Once again there was no exclusion.

But the *pièce de résistance* was saved for heat eleven, which took about as long to run as the rest of the meeting put together. New Cross's Stan Greatrex fell on the first bend and Charles and Dixon ploughed into him. The race was stopped. Charles, who was injured in the fall, was carried to the dressing room. It was announced the race would be re-run with all four riders. This was another dubious decision, given that the reason for the stoppage was quite clearly Greatrex's fall. Nothing then happened for about twelve minutes, after which time the announcer said that 'according to the rules, Frank Charles has one minute left to get ready.' The rules said that, 'In the event of a delay any rider not prepared to start within two minutes after being called on by the Steward through the announcer shall be excluded from the race.' As this was the first time Charles had been called, he should have been given two minutes, not one. Either way, Charles was not ready to start for another four minutes twenty seconds and yet the steward, Mr Alan Day, allowed the race to take place with Charles in it.

This wasn't the end of the steward's strange decisions. In the scratch race final, Dick Case fell and Smythe crashed into him. Day did not put on the red lights until the other two riders, Kilmister and Johnson, had ridden another two laps and the track was clear.

After the match the New Cross promoter, Freddie Mockford, took his protest to the control board. He complained on two grounds. The first was that Gregory should not have been allowed back onto the track once he had left it. This was dismissed by the board. The second was that Charles' 2 points should be removed as he had exceeded the time limit. This was upheld by the control board and the match score adjusted to Wembley 38 New Cross 34.

The Star Riders' Championship changed its format in 1935. Instead of each team holding preliminary rounds to find two riders to contest the final and then for that final to consist of three first round matches, three semi-finals and a final, there would now be six individual meetings run on the sixteen-rider twenty-heat individual format, each rider taking part in four of the meetings, with the top sixteen going to the final at Wembley, which would also be run on the same format. And instead of each team holding a preliminary round to find their representatives, the competitors were to be nominated by the National Speedway Association based on their past performances. Wembley had three riders nominated to take part. Lees, Kilmister and Van Praag. Before the first round started, however, as it was obvious that Lees would not return to the saddle in time, his place was taken by Charles. This was a fortuitous turn of events for the new Lion, as it later proved.

Wembley's involvement in the ACU Cup ended on 4 July as they lost at home to their nemeses, Belle Vue, by 64 points to 43. Byers was the Man of the Match as far as Wembley were concerned, scoring 12 points. Van Praag was the only other Lion to offer much resistance, gaining 11 points, and that after a point-less first heat when he was knocked off by his own partner, Smythe. During this match, Gregory became Wembley's tenth invalid of the season as he damaged an ankle and looked set to miss a few matches. Although Wembley still had one match to play, against Wimbledon, the Aces had now taken an unassailable lead.

Wembley's last ACU pool fixture saw them win comfortably against Wimbledon on the Don's home track by 62 points to 43. Once again, Byers banged in a dozen points. This final Pool One match left Belle Vue on top with 255 points, Wembley second with 209 and Wimbledon third with 175.

Having exited the ACU Cup, the Lions' next chance of cup honours was in the National Trophy. Their first round match was against West Ham and the first leg took place at Custom House on 9 July. With Gregory now out of action along with Watson, Lees and Lamont, Jackson was able to sign up a former Lion, Norman Evans, to take his place. He did not have an auspicious return, scoring just 4 points as his team went down by the rather large margin of 26 points, 67-41. Charles did his best with 12 points, but it looked as though Wembley were on their way out of this cup as well.

Although Charles with 17 points and Van Praag with 14 did their best there were just too many points to make up and, although Wembley won the return leg at the Empire Stadium 55-52, it was not enough for them to progress.

Wembley's season, which had been hit badly by injuries and illness, was virtually all over. They were out of the two major cups and, although they had staged something of a revival in the league and were currently lying in second place, they were nevertheless ten points behind Belle Vue, having raced the same number of matches, while New Cross were just two points behind them having raced two fewer fixtures. In reality the only thing left for them was the London Cup, unless one of their riders could pull off victory in a major individual trophy.

It was at this point that Kilmister seemed to suffer a complete loss of form due to a niggling injury, managing just 4 points in Wembley's 40-31 defeat at the hands of New Cross and then 3 in the Lions' 39-32 home defeat against Harringay. He was dropped to reserve to try and help him recover his confidence, but in the match against Hackney Wick he failed to score at all, even though Wembley won the match easily, 45-26, Bronco Dixon being the surprise top scorer.

A big individual event at Wembley took place on 3 August, the Wembley Gold Cup. Wembley's leading riders, including Kilmister, took part alongside top stars such as Vic Huxley, Tom Farndon, Max Grosskreutz, Bluey Wilkinson, Dicky Case, Jack Parker, Eric Langton and Bill Kitchen. The prize for first place was the cup and £300.

After heat twelve, with three rides completed each, the leaders were Grosskreutz and Wilkinson, both with an undefeated 9 points. One point behind them was Wembley's own Charles. Charles won heat thirteen to keep up the pressure as the two undefeated riders were due to meet in heat sixteen. As the tapes went up, Grosskreutz got a lightning start and was six lengths up on Wilkinson as they entered the back straight. Grosskreutz maintained his lead until the last lap. Then, entering the third bend, Wilkinson cut in, taking a sweeping dive round the inside to draw level with Grosskreutz as they came round the fourth bend. With the crowd standing on tiptoe, the pair entered the final straight shoulder to shoulder. Then, just a few yards from the winning line, Grosskreutz seemed to lose control and struck the fence, falling heavily and leaving Wilkinson to finish the race in first place. There was a storm of booing from the crowd who had the impression that the West Ham star had somehow fouled Grosskreutz. After several agonising moments, the steward switched on Wilkinson's exclusion light. With Wilkinson excluded and Grosskreutz not finishing it left the way clear for Charles. With one heat to go he now needed only one point from his final ride to ensure at least a run-off, or two points to win. Although he was up against Grosskreutz in his final ride, Charles made no mistake, winning the race in style to take the cup and the cheque. It was a fine victory over a class field for the home rider.

There was some good news for Wembley in the middle of August as George Greenwood contacted Jackson to tell him he was feeling fit again after his fall at the end of the previous season, which had so far kept him out of the saddle in 1935. A trial was arranged and, although Greenwood did not return, there was no doubt that he would be ready to start the 1936 season in the Lions' line-up.

With Wembley's reputation for making sure its riders were physically fit, the *Speedway News* decided to send one of its reporters to their gym to see what their training regime entailed. This is part of his report:

'One of the most interesting places I've been in for some time is the gymnasium at Wembley, and I must say how much I admire the spirit of the team. They take their training very seriously, and eleven o'clock every morning sees them down there stripped and really getting down to it. Dicky Smythe was skipping, Bill Lamont was having a few rounds, Jack Dixon and Gordon Byers were ball punching, Norman Evans had just finished his daily dozen, and trainer Ted Husbands was doing a spot of massaging.'

Wembley's last realistic chance of a trophy was the London Cup. The first leg of their semi-final against Harringay took place on 15 August. The match saw the return, at last, of Ginger Lees. Because he had been out for so long he was given one of the reserve spots but even so his return to the team proved to be a sad disappointment, as he took two rides and finished a poor last in both of them. The whole meeting was not good for the Lions as they lost to the Tigers by 5 points, 55–50, leaving them with a lot to do away at Green Lanes in the second leg. The one bit of good news was the return to form of Kilmister, who scored 10 points. Even so, Jackson made a curious decision in the last heat. At the time the scores were 50–49 to Wembley and the two programmed riders were Kilmister and Dixon. Dixon had won his last race but one against Ormston, who had scored 11 points for Harringay, including two heat wins, but Jackson decided to replace him with Lees, who at that point had had just one outing and was obviously nothing like his old self. Although Kilmister had been riding much better, he too was still not 100 per cent fit and so it was that the last heat finished up as a 5-1 to Harringay, giving them the victory on the night. Van Praag with 15 and Charles with 13 were Wembley's best riders.

Two nights later, in front of Harringay's biggest crowd of the season, the inevitable happened and the Tigers dumped Wembley out of the London Cup by an overall aggregate score of 121-91, winning 66-41 on their own track. Lees retained his place in the team, but once again was just a shadow of his former self, scoring 1 point.

To all intents and purposes, Wembley's season was now over. This was only confirmed the following Thursday at the Empire Stadium when once again the Lions went down to that team from the North, Belle Vue.

Lees was promoted to the team proper. His first ride did not auger well as, once again, he tailed off a bad fourth. But in his next race he scored the first victory of his comeback over Joe Abbott. Altogether he scored 5 points. Kilmister scored 6 and was obviously still not back at his best. Charles was the best of the home riders with 9 points. Belle Vue won the match 42-30 thanks, in large part, to a maximum by Grosskreutz.

Wembley's last chance of winning a major national trophy and salvaging something from the season came with the Star Riders' Championship. All three of the nominated Wembley riders, Van Praag, Charles and Kilmister, had reached the final, which was played out in the aftermath of the fatal crash at New Cross the evening before that was to take the life of one of the greatest riders of all time, Tom Farndon.

Without Farndon or Ron Johnson, who was also involved in the crash, the favourites to take the title were Max Grosskreutz, Eric Langton, Jack Parker, Bluey Wilkinson, Dicky Case and Vic Huxley. Following his victory in the Wembley Gold Cup a few weeks earlier, Charles was also seen to been in with a good chance. Wilkinson had qualified in first place with 51 points, three ahead of Farndon. Charles had qualified in tenth place with 31, just one point ahead of Kilmister. Van Praag had only just scraped in, being bottom qualifier with 24.

Grosskreutz started the meeting like an express train, breaking the track record in the very first heat to record 76.2 seconds. Not to be outdone, Charles equalled this time in the next heat, beating one of the favourites, Parker, in the process. The other two heat winners in the first round of rides were Ormston and Huxley. Grosskreutz and Ormston won their second rides. And then, in heat eight, Charles won again, beating Wilkinson and Huxley in a time of 76.4 seconds, equalling the old track record. After three rides each, Grosskreutz, Ormston and Charles remained unbeaten. Something had to give in heat fourteen as all three met. There was little doubt in the minds of the spectators that whoever won this race would also win the meeting. As they roared into the first bend, Ormston was crowded out as Grosskreutz took an early lead on Charles. It remained this way for two laps and it looked for all the world as though this race and the title would be heading the way of everything else, up north to Belle Vue. But it was not all over. Charles was piling the pressure on Grosskreutz, not letting him get away. As they entered the first bend on the third lap, Grosskreutz succumbed to the pressure and overdid it, sliding to the ground as Charles came past. Grosskreutz quickly remounted but by then it was too late, Ormston had also got past him and Charles was away, never to be caught.

After the meeting, Charles said that he knew he would need some extra effort in his race against Grosskreutz and Ormston and he guessed that Grosskreutz had the same idea as when the tapes went up they both went into the bend flat out, leaving poor Ormston stranded. He continued,

'Max is some rider, and I knew that it would take a good deal of speed and still more skill to outwit him. From the start he gained a narrow lead. I was waiting for my opportunity. It came sooner than I expected. Max took the bend too fast and over-slid, right in my path. However, I just pulled my machine round in time to clear man and machine and went on to win the race.'

The Wembley crowd were delirious. It looked as though their man would be crowned Star Riders' Champion. But before he was there was still one race each to go. With Ormston just one point behind, there was still no room for a slip-up and the Wembley fans' hearts were in their mouths as yet another Belle Vue rider, Eric Langton, gated in front of Charles in his last ride. It took Charles two laps to get past him, but get past him he did to win the trophy with an immaculate 15-point maximum.

Charles' reward was the Star Trophy and a cheque for £100, which he put towards buying a glider. It was the first time a Wembley rider had won the biggest individual trophy of them all and it was the only trophy that was to find its way to the Empire Stadium in 1935.

Not that it was of great comfort to them, but the Lions managed to score a massive 50-22 home win over New Cross. The meeting itself was a travesty of a speedway match as continuous rain had reduced the track to a soggy morass. Kilmister was the only rider who really managed to master the conditions, scoring a maximum for his team, but even he came home in one heat with a time of 97.2 seconds, approximately 20 seconds outside the track record.

Wembley also won their next match by a big score, an away tie against Wimbledon. It seemed that, too late, the team were coming together with their big three, Charles, Van Praag and Kilmister, riding the best they had ridden all season while Smythe, Byers and Dixon were giving strong support as the second strings. The only weak member of the team was Lees, who was still not really fully fit following his long lay-off and, just as the management had feared when he was first injured, Lees decided it was no longer worth his while to race; he consequently announced his retirement from the sport after the Empire Stadium's next meeting, the Wembley Grand Prix. There was some speculation about who would take his place as former rider Harry Whitfield was seen talking to some of his former teammates at the meeting but Whitfield quickly put paid to any rumours, announcing that he was now a respectable businessman and had decided against doing any more hard work!

The Grand Prix proved to be yet another triumph for Charles as he scored a hat-trick of successes in big meetings at Wembley. This time he beat Langton and Case into second and third places respectively. His prize was a brand new bike. After being presented with his prize by Mrs Jackson, the announcer got very excited, announcing, 'I am sure we would all like to congratulate Frank Charles, who will now ride round the track on his astounding feat.' On being interviewed by the Press following his third successive individual meeting win, Charles admitted to still being disappointed as he could only get his Aston Martin car to do 94mph and he wanted to do a hundred.

Wembley continued their end-of-season winning ways, beating West Ham 45-25, with Charles contributing a maximum. The run came to an end with their very last match of the season, however, as they went down to Harringay 43-28. But in any case, their short revival had been too little too late and they had to settle for fourth place in the league.

For Wembley the season's end couldn't come too quickly and it was definitely a season to forget. Greenwood didn't even start the season due to his injury in 1934, then within the first two weeks they had lost Watson and Lees. Charles and Lamont had been signed up as top-class replacements – Lamont never made the grade, while Charles eventually did, but even he was ill and missed a few matches. Kilmister was also injured during the season, along with Gregory and Smythe. On the plus side, Byers and Dixon were ever-presents, as was Van Praag, who assumed the captaincy on Lees' injury. This added responsibility seemed to be just what he needed and he improved his average to 7.79 as against 7.23 the previous season. Of course, the signing of Charles was Jackson's masterstroke. By the end of the season he had become one of the country's leading riders and Star Riders' Champion.

Just as the season came to a close, Greenwood was pronounced fit to ride by his doctor after nearly eighteen months of inactivity. Perhaps it was the first sign that things would be better for the Lions in 1936.

1935 National League Averages – qualification 6 matches

	Matches	Rides	Points	BP	Total	CMA
Frank Charles	20	80	166	8	174	8.70
Wally Kilmister	19	72	143	8	151	8.39
Lionel Van Praag	24	96	177	10	187	7.79
Gordon Byers	24	95	119	26	145	6.11
Jack 'Bronco' Dixon	24	76	96	12	108	5.68
Eric Gregory	14	46	43	15	58	5.04
Dick Smythe	21	60	57	14	71	4.73

National League Matches

Date	H/A	Against	W/L/D	Score
30 April	Away	West Ham	Lost	31-40
9 May	Home	Wimbledon	Lost	35-36
11 May	Away	Belle Vue	Lost	25-46
16 May	Home	Harringay	Won	41-31
17 May	Away	Hackney Wick	Lost	28-43
23 May	Home	West Ham	Lost	28-42
30 May	Home	Belle Vue	Won	37-34
1 June	Away	Harringay	Lost	30-41
3 June	Away	Wimbledon	Won	41-29
12 June	Away	New Cross	Won	38-34
20 June	Home	Hackney Wick	Won	42-28
22 June	Away	Belle Vue	Lost	23-49
27 June	Home	New Cross	Won	39-33
18 July	Home	Wimbledon	Won	48-22
24 July	Away	New Cross	Won	39-33
25 July	Home	Harringay	Lost	32-39
8 August	Home	Hackney Wick	Won	45-26
22 August	Home	Belle Vue	Lost	30-42
26 August	Away	Hackney Wick	Lost	32-40
5 September	Home	New Cross	Won	50-22

7 September	Away	Wimbledon	Won	46-25
10 September	Away	West Ham	Lost	31-41
19 September	Home	West Ham	Won	45-25
12 October	Away	Harringay	Lost	28-43

National League Table

	Played	Won	Drawn	Lost	For	Against	Points
Belle Vue	24	18	2	4	957	752	38
Harringay	24	13	0	11	874.5	823.5	26
West Ham	24	12	1	11	856	852	25
WEMBLEY	24	11	0	13	855	852	22
Hackney Wick	24	10	1	13	824.5	879.5	21
New Cross	24	10	0	14	822	889	20
Wimbledon	24	8	0	16	780	921	16

National Trophy

First Round
West Ham 67 Wembley 41
Wembley 55 West Ham 52
Aggregate: West Ham 119 Wembley 96

ACU Cup

Pool One
Wembley 43 Belle Vue 64
Wembley 72 Wimbledon 35
Belle Vue 74 Wimbledon 34
Wimbledon 43 Wembley 62
Final Race Points
Belle Vue 255
Wembley 211
Wimbledon 175

London Cup

First Round
Wembley: Bye

Semi-Final
Harringay 66 Wembley 41
Wembley 50 Harringay 55
Aggregate: Harringay 121 Wembley 91

NO. 4 – FRANK CHARLES

Frank Charles was born on 10 March 1908 in Barrow-in-Furness. His first job was in the family baking business but he thought this was 'boring' and he became a professional piano-accordionist in the music halls. By this time he was already an accomplished motorcyclist, having first learned to ride motorcycles in beach races around the northern seaside resorts. When the speedway craze hit the country, Charles decided to have a go. His first ride was at Blackpool. Although he had never even seen speedway before, he won his first race – but was promptly disqualified for looking behind! After his success at Blackpool the lure of the speedway became too strong to resist and he was soon thrilling the crowds at Manchester White City, Belle Vue, Burnley, Preston and Leeds.

The life as a piano-accordionist had begun to pall. The final straw was when he was booked to appear as an interval attraction in cinemas. Sitting through the same film time after time waiting to go on bored him and he quit to take up speedway full time. Unfortunately, in 1931, while riding for Leeds, he was involved in a bad accident at the Leicester Super track and he was unable to race again for a long time and returned to the family bakery business.

It wasn't until 1933, by which time he had become a forgotten name on the speedway, that the Belle Vue team manager, E.O. Spence, prevailed upon Charles to take up the sport again. After just a few weeks of reacclimatising, it was as though he had never been away. He linked up with Joe Abbott and the pair were so successful that they began to earn a reputation as the best pair in the country. By the end of the following season he was averaging 8.60.

Towards the end of 1934, Charles' father died. Charles senior was an expert mechanic and had accompanied his son to all his matches, looking after his bikes. With the death of his father, Charles decided to quit the sport and instead went into the grocery business.

He was persuaded back into the sport by Jackson, who paid a record £1,000 transfer fee for his services. Barely a fortnight after his return he was named for the first Test against Australia at Wembley and scored 11 points. In his first season for Wembley, 1935, he became the team's top scorer and star rider as he won several individual championships, culminating in the Star Riders' Championship at Wembley.

He once again topped the Wembley averages in 1936, this time with a double-figure average. Although he had to play second-fiddle to Van Praag in 1937 and 1938, he was still a major force, failing to score paid double-figure scores on just four occasions in 1937.

Frank Charles.

At the end of the 1938 season he decided to retire to concentrate on gliding, but he didn't stay away for long and made a comeback on 15 June 1939. The reception given him on his reappearance was one of the warmest ever given to a Wembley rider at the Empire Stadium. Although he had not ridden since the end of the previous season, he scored 10 points.

His piano-accordion skills came in useful at Wembley as he entertained the crowds during the intervals and also at the supporters' club dances.

He qualified for the 1936 World Championship final, finishing in fourth place, and the 1937 final, finishing sixth. Altogether he rode in twenty-one Test matches for England, scoring 179 points.

Although he was very committed to speedway, his real love was gliding. 'Like every other rider,' he once said, 'I should like to win the World Championship, but I am far more concerned with beating gliding records. And I must say that if I can earn enough on the speedway to be able to build thousands of gliders I shall be satisfied.' But gliding was as dangerous a sport as speedway. He crashed several times, including once near his home town of Barrow when he landed on the edge of a cliff in a quarry. And it was gliding that finally did for him. The crash that killed Charles came on 15 July 1939 in the national gliding competition at Great Hucklow, Derbyshire. The tow line had failed to fall free from his glider at around 300 feet and the sailplane nosedived into the ground, killing Frank instantly. Charles had been selected to ride for England in a Test match at Harringay that night but asked to be excused so he could take part in the gliding competition. Tragically, the England selectors agreed to release him.

NINE

1936 – SO NEAR AND YET...

During the winter months the Wembley team members went their various ways. Byers and Gregory were to be found at work – Byers in his father's garage and Gregory selling electric hair-waving machines. Charles returned to his great love, gliding, while Van Praag, Lamont and Kilmister returned home to carry on racing. Kilmister in particular had a good year, winning the New Zealand Championship and scoring a 'maximum' in an unofficial Test match, consisting of four heats, against America. Greenwood spent the winter practising at High Beech and in the car park at Wembley, which had to be rolled every day because he used it to practice his clutch starts. Smythe took to the ice and became a proficient ice skater. Watson worked in his shop, a sports outfitters, but still harboured hopes of a return to the saddle. He was due to be operated on at Easter when a plate, inserted when the original fracture occurred, was to be removed from his leg.

Just before the 1936 season started, Jackson declared his contracted riders to be Van Praag, Lees, Kilmister, Greenwood, Gregory, Bowden, Charles, Watson, Byers and Lamont. Wally Lloyd was signed up and, in a surprise move, Jackson announced that he had tempted veteran Roger Frogley (Buster's brother) out of retirement, mainly to coach the juniors but also ready to be called upon to ride if needed. One further signing was the South African champion, Cecil de la Porte. One rider went the other way as Smythe was transferred to Harringay. Jackson was also still carefully nurturing his juniors and both Millward and Tommy Price were loaned out to Provincial League clubs for the season to gain more experience, Millward to Nottingham and Price to Cardiff.

Price had been riding on a number of training circuits, such as Barnet, and had had a trial for Harringay, but had been rejected in favour of George Wilks. He also had some second-half outings at Luton where Wembley's reserve team rode their matches. One day he noticed that a friend of his who rode in the reserve team, George Hannaford, looked unwell and asked the doctor to take a look at him. It transpired that Hannaford had been walking about for several days with a fractured skull! As the reserves were due to race the following day, Price telephoned Jackson to tell him that Hannaford was unable to ride. Jackson asked him if he could deputise. Price was delighted to oblige and in his first meeting turned out to be the highest scorer of the day. Jackson then included Price in the Novices' second-half race at Wembley itself and he won six weeks on the trot.

The 1936 Wembley team. From left to right, back row: Wally Lloyd, Eric Gregory, Frank Charles, Alec Jackson (manager), Ginger Lees, Gordon Byers, George Greenwood. Front row: Cliff Parkinson, Lionel Van Praag.

There was some concern about whether Lamont would show up. Before leaving for Australia at the back end of 1935, he said he would definitely return and hoped that his form would improve the following year. By the start of the 1936 season, however, the only communication they had had from him was a Christmas card that read, 'With love and kisses, Bill.'

To put in a real challenge for the various trophies on offer and to try to end Belle Vue's dominance of the sport, Jackson knew he had to try and persuade Lees to end his retirement. He therefore paid a visit to the Lees home in April. His own description of the meeting was that he spent eight-and-a-quarter hours with the Lees family and for seven-and-three-quarter hours nothing happened. After eight hours, Lees began to consider the possibility and after eight-and-a-quarter hours the job was done.

There was no change to the League set-up this year, with the same seven teams contesting the National League. Wembley's first match was a friendly away to New Cross. It was a good victory for the Lions as they won 39-33. Charles, Kilmister and Van Praag all shone, with Charles in particular restarting the season where he left off the last. The other three members of the team were Byers, Lloyd and Gregory. It was a promising start.

Also encouraging was the form of the three stars in early season open meetings and second-half scratch races at various tracks. In particular, Charles won the Manchester Cup, deep in the heart of enemy territory at Belle Vue, after a titanic struggle with Grosskreutz in the final. It was noted that all three of the Wembley heat leaders were showing 'astonishing acceleration and steadiness at the bends' (*Speedway News* 25 April 1936). Much of this good work was being put down to their machinery and in particular Wembley's chief mechanic, Cyril Spinks, who had been working throughout the winter at the indoor workshop. Jackson had introduced a new machine to the workshop called a Dynomometer. This was something unique to Wembley that registered the revs per minute and recorded the bhp readings. Jackson insisted that every engine was tested on the machine. As well as making sure the machinery was in the best possible condition, Jackson was once again insisting on a strict training regime to make sure the riders were also at peak fitness. There was compulsory training on two days a week under Husbands. A fine of 10s was imposed on any rider who failed to put in an appearance on a training day.

Wembley's league campaign opened at West Ham on 28 April. It was a triumph for the Lions, who hammered the Hammers 45-27 with a good all-round team effort. Kilmister and Charles each scored 10 paid 11, while Byers contributed 8 paid 10, Van Praag 6 paid 7 and Lloyd 5 paid 6 from three rides. Even the reserve, Gregory, did well, scoring 2 paid 3 from two rides. The only disappointment was Lees, who managed just 4 points from three rides. It was obvious to everyone that he had still not recovered from his injury and long lay-off.

With the Lions winning their second match, also away from home, at Wimbledon, it seemed to many that Wembley were back where they belonged and would be a force to be reckoned with in the coming season. Once again, Charles and Van Praag rode well, but the rider who won it for the Lions was Lees. Although still not quite back to his best, he managed to score 10 points. If he could keep up this improvement and return to his 1934 form, Wembley would have four riders – Lees, Charles, Van Praag and Kilmister – of heat-leader class and with Byers and Lloyd to support them they were beginning to look like favourites for the league title again.

One of the major aspects of their three winning performances was their starting technique. The whole team had been drilled by Jackson into perfecting this and in nearly every heat it was the two Lions riders who left the gate as if shot out of a gun. It was this meticulous attention to detail – care of the bikes, physical training, technical coaching, looking after the juniors – that marked Wembley out from the rest. Jackson did not like to leave anything to chance. He wanted to make the name Wembley respected throughout the speedway world as it was in every other sport. In this he was supported by Elvin, who wanted the same and to whom money was no object.

Although Greenwood was fit enough to ride again he could not get into the team, especially now that Lees was back. But he kept his hand in by riding on the Continent, where he was very successful, waiting for the day when he would be recalled. There was one further addition to the team before Wembley's opening match at the Empire Stadium on 7 May as Cliff Parkinson was brought in from Hackney Wick as rider/mechanic.

Wembley's opening meeting proved to be a shock to the whole speedway world as, after their great start to the season, the Lions lost at home to Wimbledon by 38 points to 33. To add insult to injury, Grosskreutz took the Cinders Trophy in the second half, beating the one-lap track record with a time of 18.2 seconds.

The following week the Lions lost at home again, this time to their bitter rivals Belle Vue, and this in spite of a twelve-point maximum from Charles. Unfortunately, he received no real support., Van Praag and Kilmister being next highest scorers with 5 each.

Two nights later and another loss came, this time at Harringay, as the Lions went down 39-33. Once again it was Charles who saved the team from a complete rout, scoring 9 points from his first three rides and then suffering engine failure in his last.

Jackson was fast becoming a very worried man. Kilmister had suddenly seemed to go completely off the boil. After a good start to the season his form had plummeted, while Lees was still nowhere near fit enough to last out a whole match. Van Praag had not made the progress he was expecting either and the whole team was now being carried on the shoulders of Charles.

With the first 'pool' match in the ACU Cup approaching, Jackson had a lot of work to do. He had the team in for special training sessions, discussed tactics and had Spinks put every bike through its paces in the workshop. The result of all this was that on 21 May, Wembley thumped Wimbledon by 59 points to 37. In truth, however, there was an element of 'papering over the cracks' in the victory. Charles, naturally, was top scorer with 11 paid 12, but it was the return of Greenwood to the team at reserve and the performance of second strings, Gregory and Byers that really turned the tide for the Lions, although Kilmister rode better for his 7 points. But after his first race win, Lees once again quickly tired and added only one more point to his total in later races, while Van Praag scored just 5.

The return ACU Cup match at Plough Lane followed two days later. It was a close call, but once again Wembley made it, this time by four points, 49-45, with Charles scoring a maximum. Kilmister's return to form continued as he picked up three race wins, although once again it was Byers and Greenwood who added the necessary solidity in the middle order to make up for the poor showing of Lees and Van Praag.

It was a return to the league for their next match and this time it was a much more convincing victory for the Lions, away at Hackney Wick. Kilmister, back to his best, top scored with 11, while Van Praag showed flashes of his early season form as he weighed in with 9.

It was back to the ACU Cup for the next encounter and it looked as though the blip in form was now well and truly behind them as the Lions raced to a 59-37 win away to New Cross. In fact, such was the return to form of the Wembley team that the match turned into a monotonous procession of Lions victories, if not 5-1s, then certainly 4-2s. Charles scored a maximum and Kilmister dropped just one point. But much better from Jackson's point of view was the fact that Van Praag was also right back to form with a maximum while Lees too only dropped one point. Perhaps, at last, his four heat-leader spearhead was coming together and he could put the inexplicable recent loss of form amoungst his top riders – Charles excepted of course – behind him.

The return back at the Empire Stadium confirmed this view as, once again, the Lions beat New Cross, this time 54-42. Charles scored yet another maximum, while Van Praag scored 9 from three heats and then reared at the start of his last race. Lees scored 10. The result of these four pool matches meant that Wembley were through to the final of the ACU Cup. And with the team performing the way they were, there was every expectation that they would go on to win it.

With the four stars now back on form and Byers, Lloyd and Gregory giving good support, Jackson loaned out Lamont, who had eventually returned to England, to Plymouth and Greenwood to Nottingham.

More cup success followed as Wembley took on and beat Wimbledon over two legs in the National Trophy. A 61-47 win at home was followed by an even bigger 65-42 victory away. Charles scored 18-point maximums in both matches, while Van Praag also scored a maximum in the second leg and 14 in the first. For Charles this meant that in the six cup ties raced so far this season – four ACU Cup and two National Trophy – he had dropped just one point.

Another big victory followed, this time in the league at home to Hackney, by 43 points to 29. Charles had the unusual experience of not scoring a maximum as in heat four he got tangled up with his partner, Byers, and both fell. He was not excluded but was unable to take part in the re-run. Once again it was a good all-round performance with Van Praag and Lees top scoring with 9. There were great scenes in the second half of the meeting as Lamont came out to take part in the first round of the stadium scratch race (for reserves). There were loud cheers from all round the ground as Lamont went on to win his heat and then the final, beating Price into second place.

Wembley's purple patch came to an abrupt end on 27 June at Belle Vue as they were defeated by the Mancunian team 41–30. They also suffered three injuries in the match. Kilmister fell in heat two and was out for the rest of the meeting, his place being taken by Lamont, while Charles over-slid in heat nine, having won his first two races. For some reason the steward failed to switch on the red lights even though Charles' bike was still on the track and, coming round on the next lap, Byers crashed in to it. Both were out for the rest of the meeting. Lees tried his best, putting in two wins, but with Kilmister, Charles and Byers all out there was no chance of the Lions getting the better of the Aces.

Before further team racing could take place, all the Wembley riders took part in the new competition that had been introduced this year, the World Championship. At the beginning of the season, the ACU had announced its introduction with a first prize of £500 for the winner and the title World Champion. It was to take the place of the Star Riders' Championship and the British Individual Championship. Sixty-three riders from eleven different countries entered. Preliminary rounds were held on most tracks in the country, National League and Provincial League, with the top twenty-eight competitors going through to the next round with heats being held on each of the National League tracks, with every rider riding in four heats. From there sixteen riders would qualify for the final itself, to be held at the Empire Stadium. As no rider was allowed to ride on his home track in the preliminary round, the Wembley round resulted in a win for the New Cross captain Ron Johnson. There was such a wide variation in class between the riders that racing in all the heats was fairly poor. The *Speedway News* journalist reporting on the Wembley round said that 'One or two races provided thrills just in time to prevent a universal demand for black coffee – hot and strong!' It did give the Wembley spectators the opportunity of seeing the Swedish champion, Torsten Sjoberg, but he did not fare well and failed to qualify for the next round. Three Wembley riders qualified for the next round, Charles (with maximum points), Van Praag and Lees. Lloyd and Byers just missed out and were allocated reserve positions.

With Kilmister and Charles still suffering from the injuries sustained at Belle Vue, it was a weakened Lions side that took on Wimbledon on the latter's home track but, thanks to maximums from Lees and Van Praag, Wembley just scraped a victory by one point, 36–35. Lamont and Parkinson were brought into the team but scored only three points between them. The reserve spot was taken by the young Wembley junior Tommy Price and, although he was not called upon to ride, it was the first time he had made the first-team team-sheet.

Following this match, the Wembley team once again went away for a week's get-together, this time on the Norfolk Broads where Jackson had ordered a yacht for them. But, as in the previous year's trip to 'somewhere near Folkestone', the get-together was no holiday and the whole team were put through a rigorous programme of physical training by Husbands.

The team returned in time for four of them to be chosen for their respective sides in the third Test at Belle Vue, which England won 70–38. Charles was top scorer for England with 16 while Van Praag was top scorer for Australia with 11. Lees and Lamont were picked as reserves.

With the team back to full strength for the next home match they were too much for West Ham. Van Praag was in magnificent form and scored a maximum, Charles scored a paid maximum and Lees contributed 8 and had one engine failure. Gregory and Byers added a useful 5 points each. The final score was Wembley 43 West Ham 28. In the second half, Charles took the Cinders Trophy, knocking 0.4 of a second off Grosskreutz's time to record 18.2 seconds.

Always on the look-out to create publicity for the team, the Wembley management produced twelve photographs of their riders and put them on sale in an envelope for 6d the set. Two thousand were put on sale for the first time at the West Ham match. Within an hour the whole lot had been sold.

Wembley's forgotten man, Colin Watson, was a visitor to the West Ham match. He let it be known that he was feeling fit enough to start practising again and hoped to be racing properly before the season finished. There was one slight drawback to this plan, however, as he had sold all his equipment when he realised he would be out of the saddle for a long period.

Another good victory followed, this time away at New Cross. Once again Van Praag scored a maximum, with Charles adding 10 paid 11 and Lees 9. The recent run of wins put Wembley in second place in the league with 14 points from 11 matches. Belle Vue were top with 20 points from 12.

Van Praag's excellent form continued into the next Test match at Wimbledon where, once again, he was the Australians' top scorer, with 15 points. When the riders' league averages for the end of July were published he had in fact risen from fourteenth place at the end of May to sixth. Charles was in second place behind Jack Parker.

The ACU Cup final was next for Wembley. Unsurprisingly, they were once again taking on Belle Vue. The first leg was at the Empire Stadium and resulted in a narrow win for the Lions, 48-47. Charles scored 11, while Van Praag scored 9 from three rides, suffering engine problems in his fourth. Price made his racing debut for the Lions, scoring 1 point.

Perhaps the strangest race of the season occurred in heat seven. Belle Vue's Tommy Price (oddly, there was a Tommy Price in each team) fell on the first bend but the race continued. Byers and Gregory led coming out of the second bend with Bill Kitchen hot on their heels. On the second lap Byers' motor conked out, leaving Gregory to fight it out with Kitchen. On the third lap Kitchen made a supreme effort and passed Gregory to give Belle Vue a 3-2 lead in the race. With just over half a lap to go, Gregory's motor also packed up and he freewheeled onto the centre green, parking his machine there while Kitchen went on to finish the race alone. After the chequered flag fell, the tractor came out to grade the track and, while it tootled round, pushers-off came to fetch Gregory's machine. While everyone was busy filling in their programmes, Gregory waved away the helpers and started to push the bike himself, taking it back onto the track and pushing it towards the finishing line, seemingly in a race with the tractor while having to avoid the rakers as he went. He eventually crossed the line and gained two points for his team. A vital two points as it turned out, given the final score.

Thirty thousand spectators witnessed the second leg at Hyde Road. With just a slender one-point lead, it looked hopeless for the Lions, but they managed to fight the Aces all the way. ACU Cup matches were sixteen heats and at the end of heat fourteen the aggregate scores were level. But heat fifteen more or less ended their chances as Abbott and Varey scored a 5-1. There was still a slim chance of a draw if Wembley could return the favour in the last heat, but Kitchen got away first from the tapes and was never headed, though Charles was right behind him every inch of the way. Charles and Van Praag were once again the pick of the Lions with 11 and 10 points respectively.

The following Thursday, Wembley held its second round of the World Championship. The headline after the meeting was, 'Van Praag after that £500?' It was expected that Charles would clean up on his own track, but it was Van Praag who took the full 15 points instead. The general opinion of him was that he rode like a 'world-beater' and was fast becoming one of the leading

World Champion Lionel Van Praag.

favourites to take the World title. In second place was Huxley with 13 points. In the end, Charles managed just 9 points, the same as Lees.

The Lions were back at Belle Vue for their next match, this time the first leg of the National Trophy semi-final. It was a massacre. In a very one-sided meeting, the Aces crushed Wembley by 78 points to 30. Van Praag, with 11 points, and Lees with 10, scored 21 of the Lions' 30 points between them. Charles seemed to be right off form, sluggish from the tapes and without the fighting spirit to make up the ground lost.

The result of the semi-final was a foregone conclusion, but the Lions managed to salvage some pride in the second leg by beating Belle Vue, even if it was by just one point, 54-53. Van Praag showed why he had become a favourite to take the world title by scoring a maximum 18. The young Price showed up well and, in one race, took the formidable Aces skipper Eric Langton all the way to the wire, losing by just a few inches. Unfortunately, he was also injured in a fall in the match, sustaining concussion that put him out for a while. This did not stop several promoters ringing up Jackson and asking if the young man was for sale. Jackson firmly rejected all offers, as he felt he may have another world beater on his hands.

The next night, Wembley recorded a good victory at Waterden Road, home of the Hackney Wick Wolves, beating them 42-30. The four top riders seemed to be back to their best, but it was once again Van Praag who stole the show, scoring a twelve-point maximum as well as winning his heat and the final of the second-half scratch race.

Although the World Championship was fast approaching, Charles had his mind on other things as he attempted to beat the existing British gliding record of ninety-five miles, set in 1934. He built himself a new glider weighing 300lbs and was hoping that, with the right wind behind him, he could set a new record somewhere in the region of 200 miles. He proposed making this attempt near his home in Barrow-in-Furness.

Wembley continued their winning ways in the league with an important victory over Belle Vue, 37-34. With the Lions three points in front with one heat to go, it all depended on the last heat. But even with Grosskreutz and Langton out for the Aces, Van Praag was able to ensure victory and two points for Wembley.

The following week it was Charles's turn to outdo Van Praag as he scored the only maximum of the match in the Lions' 43-28 victory over West Ham. In both these matches the heat-leader trio of Van Praag, Charles and Lees performed well, but there was great concern about Kilmister, who contributed just 1 and 3 points. Two days later, in the 45-27 defeat at the hands of Belle Vue, he did even worse, failing to score at all. Jackson was very worried about the form of his fourth heat leader and after a further point-less match by the New Zealander, against New Cross, he was dropped to reserve, but he did no better there, contributing just 1 point in his next two league matches.

It was just as well for Wembley that Gregory started turning in a few points at home: 8 against West Ham on 13 August and 8 paid 11 against Harringay the following week. These points enabled the Lions to remain strong at home but away from home they were losing too many matches to look as though they would be in a position to seriously challenge Belle Vue. The defeat at New Cross, 42-30 on 19 August, was typical. Charles with 9, Van Praag with paid 9 and Lees with 7 all did their bit but the next highest scorer was Byers with 3. Kilmister, once again failed to score. Van Praag's total of paid 9 came from just three races as he was excluded for boring in his other.

There was some good news on the individual front to cheer up the faithful Lions supporters a few days later as Greenwood won the Provincial League Riders' Championship and the final Test match scorecard showed that Charles was top scorer for England with 68 points, while Van Praag was top for Australia with 57.

Kilmister made an unexpected, if welcome, return to form on 3 September as he contributed 12 points to Wembley's 60-47 win over Harringay in the first leg of the London Cup semi-final. Van Praag top scored with 16.

Back to the bread and butter of league racing and the Wembley team kept alive their slender hopes of taking the title by defeating West Ham at Custom House on 8 September. It was another good night for Charles and Van Praag, who scored 11 and 10 respectively. Kilmister managed to win one race but only added one more point to that.

Van Praag's form over the past couple of months had been nothing short of sensational. He had regularly turned in double-figure scores, including four full league maximums on the trot between 27 June and 31 July. This, combined with his form in the World Championship qualifying rounds, had made him one of the favourites to take the title. Charles was another favourite. His record in individual meetings at Wembley spoke for itself and his ability to mix it with the very best in the sport was never in doubt.

The World Championship final was held on 10 September in front of a record 74,000-strong crowd at the Empire Stadium, beating the record of 70,000 set at the 1932 Wembley Test match.

Three Wembley riders qualified for the final, Charles in second place with 59 points, seven behind Langton's 66; Van Praag in fifth place with 58 and Lees in fourteenth place with 37.

Controversially, a bonus points system had been introduced into the World Championship, so that riders took with them into the final points based on how well they had done in the two qualifying rounds. Under this system, Langton took 13 points into the final, Charles and Van Praag 12 and Lees 7. The fact was that Lees had more or less no chance of becoming World Champion even if he won every race. Charles and Van Praag, on the other hand, had everything to race for.

Charles started off like an express train, winning his first heat in a new track record time of 73.6 seconds. Van Praag also won his first heat as did Langton, the rider they needed to gain a point over if they were to win the title.

It was the same story in the second round of rides as Charles, Van Praag and Langton all won. Wilkinson, with a bonus tally of 10, also won his first two rides. After the first two rides each, therefore, the scores were Langton 19, Charles and Van Praag 18, Wilkinson 16.

Heat nine saw the two Wembley riders up against each other. Many felt this could well be the deciding race of the championship as if they both beat Langton, the winner of this race would have made up sufficient points to take the title. As the tapes went up, Van Praag was off like a bullet but Charles missed the gate completely and by the time he had recovered he was struggling in fourth place. He never made up the ground and his championship was all over. Not so for Van Praag, however, as he crossed the line in first place to maintain his unbeaten record. Frustratingly for him, Langton also won his third race, as did Wilkinson.

Heat thirteen saw two of the night's unbeaten riders up against each other as Langton took on Wilkinson. Much to Van Praag's relief, Wilkinson took the chequered flag and Langton had lost his one-point-bonus lead. But, in the very next heat, Wilkinson did the same to Van Praag, so they were back where they had been before, with Langton holding a one-point lead thanks to the bonus. The very last heat of the championship now became crucial. It was Van Praag against Langton. Van Praag had to beat Langton and even then he would only equal him on points and a run-off would be needed. When Van Praag duly took the heat, the stage was set for one of the most tense and exciting races of the season to find the first ever speedway World Champion.

Van Praag had been preparing for months for this occasion. He had arrived in England five years ago with a good reputation but had taken some time to fulfil it. At the beginning of 1935 he had been handed the Wembley captaincy and it seemed to change his attitude to the sport. He had begun to take his responsibilities more seriously, training hard and making sure his equipment was always immaculate. The result of this was that his riding had improved and now here he was, just one race away from the pinnacle of speedway fame. Nevertheless, he had a very calm temperament and, at times like this, it proved invaluable. Langton, on the other hand, was a more nervous character and seemed very anxious as they prepared in the pits for the run-off. As they came up to the tapes, this anxiety manifested itself as Langton jumped the start, breaking the tapes. Both riders circled round and came back up to the tapes. Once again, Langton beat Van Praag from the start, only this time it was legal, and he led into the first bend. He kept his lead round the first lap but Van Praag's ice-cold disposition paid off as he kept at Langton. It was just a momentary lapse of concentration on Langton's part, but it was enough and Van Praag was through. For three more pulsating laps, Langton tried everything he knew to regain the lead, but Van Praag was not going to have his chance of glory in front of his own supporters taken

Lionel Van Praag being presented with the World Championship trophy. On the left is runner-up Eric Langton.

away from him and he blocked every move Langton tried. As they took the chequered flag there was less than a length in it, but that length was in Van Praag's favour. The Wembley captain had brought back the biggest prize in speedway, and against the Belle Vue captain of all people!

Van Praag had won because he combined all the necessary qualifications of a world speedway champion. He had the inherent riding ability, sedulously improved by careful study of the sport and of his opponents. He had the keen brain that many of his rivals overlooked to their peril. He had the temperament to produce his best on even the biggest of occasions and he had the physique to withstand the demands of six hard-fought races in a single night. He also had considerable mechanical skill, which he used to find the best possible set-up for his bike.

It was not such a good night for the other Wembley riders. After his brilliant start, Charles faded and finished the evening with just two more points from his last three rides, while Lees could only manage a total of four to add to his bonus score.

Although Van Praag had done what he needed to win, there were many who felt his victory a rather hollow one as there was no doubt that he was not the best rider on view that night. West Ham's Australian, Bluey Wilkinson, had gone through the card undefeated but because of the quirks of the bonus system could only finish in overall third place, one point behind Van Praag and Langton. Many argued that this proved that the bonus system was untenable but nothing was done about it and it remained in force until the World Championship was revived after the Second World War in 1949.

After his success in the World Championship, Van Praag was called on to endorse a wide variety of products, including, as shown here, egg flip.

Following the excitement of the World Championship final, Wembley travelled to Green Lanes for the second leg of the London Cup semi-final tie. With a 13-point lead from the first leg, the Lions were expected to make it to the final where they would meet surprise qualifiers Hackney Wick, a team they had already beaten home and away this year. But Harringay had not read the script as they overcame the deficit and went on to win by 19 points, 63-44, to give them victory by an aggregate 110 points to 104. The problem for Wembley came in the very first heat, as their new World Champion reared at the start and his machine went right over. Although he rode for the rest of the evening it was a very different Van Praag to the one of just two days earlier. Charles with 16 and Lees with 13 tried their best but there was no real backing. Once again Kilmister failed, scoring just 1 point. Wembley had now lost their last chance of a cup and had just the league left to aim for, and that too was beginning to look a lost cause.

A narrow one-point victory over New Cross in their next match kept that slender hope alive. Van Praag was not well and did not ride. Byers was promoted to heat leader, with his place being taken by Lloyd, while Price was brought into the team as reserve. As the riders went into the last race, Wembley were, in fact, one point behind but a 4-2 to Charles and Kilmister gave them the result they needed by 36 points to 35. Charles and Lees both scored 11.

Just one week after losing in the London Cup semi-final, the Lions found themselves back at Green Lanes in a make-or-break league match. To have any chance at all of overhauling Belle Vue they had to win the encounter as they were seven points behind with four matches to race.

Van Praag was still unwell and his place was again taken by Byers, with Lloyd promoted to the team. This time it was old Wembley favourite George Greenwood who put in an appearance at reserve. In a bad-tempered match, the Tigers beat the Lions by an even bigger margin, 45-26. Wembley won only two heats all night, both wins coming from Charles, who finished with 10 points. The bad tempers came about because Jackson complained about the state of the track, to which he put down his team's loss, and he refused to allow his riders to race in the second half. The Harringay promoter, Tom Bradbury-Pratt, lodged a formal protest against Wembley and demanded a full-scale inquiry by the control board. It took the board two meetings to decided that there had been a breach of the regulations. All the Wembley riders were fined £10 each and Jackson £25. However, they also found that the Harringay track had not been maintained sufficiently and ordered that Bradbury-Pratt bring it up to standard immediately.

Whatever the reason for Wembley's loss at Harringay, it was the final nail in the coffin as far as any hope of a title in 1936 went. On the same night as Wembley lost to Harringay, Belle Vue crushed Wimbledon by 55 points to 17. This was Belle Vue's last fixture and meant that they had finished with 37 points. Wembley still had three matches to race but were now 9 points behind.

In the end it didn't matter very much how far they were behind as they managed to lose two of their remaining fixtures, all of which were at home. For the match against Hackney Wick on 24 September, which the Lions lost 44-28, Price was again brought in as reserve as Greenwood was promoted to heat leader to take Van Praag's place and scored his first ever race win for Wembley over Dick Case and Baltzar Hansen.

The final league match of the season ended in a bittersweet irony for Wembley as they finally overcame the team that had been giving them so many problems at the latter end of the season, Harringay. Price was promoted to the team proper for this match but only scored 1 point. It was a fitting end for the three heat leaders though, as both Van Praag and Charles scored maximums and Lees added 10.

In the second half of the meeting, Watson made a return to the track and said he hoped to be fit enough to win his place back in the team for 1937. Lees, on the other hand, announced at the meeting that this would be his last and that he had no intention of returning for 1937.

In fact, Jackson was so disappointed by his team's performance at the latter end of the season that he decided only Van Praag, Charles and Gregory would definitely be offered places the following year.

The Lions had almost forgotten what it was like to win a trophy. This is not what Sir Arthur Elvin wanted for a team that bore the proud name of Wembley. He told Jackson he hoped for more success in 1937. Jackson had a lot of team building to do.

1936 National League Averages – qualification 6 matches

	Matches	Rides	Points	BP	Total	CMA
Frank Charles	23	90	221	4	225	10.00
Lionel Van Praag	21	83	191	5	196	9.45
Ginger Lees	24	95	180	10	190	8.00
Gordon Byers	23	86	88	26	114	5.30

Wally Kilmister	18	59	69	6	75	5.08
Eric Gregory	22	82	81	22	103	5.02
Wally Lloyd	18	53	44	10	54	4.08

National League Matches

Date	H/A	Against	W/L/D	Score
28 April	Away	West Ham	Won	45-27
2 May	Away	Wimbledon	Won	37-34
7 May	Home	Wimbledon	Lost	33-38
14 May	Home	Belle Vue	Lost	32-40
16 May	Away	Harringay	Lost	33-39
29 May	Away	Hackney Wick	Won	42-30
18 June	Home	Hackney Wick	Won	43-29
20 June	Away	Belle Vue	Lost	30-41
27 June	Away	Wimbledon	Won	36-35
2 July	Home	West Ham	Won	43-28
8 July	Away	New Cross	Won	43-28
31 July	Away	Hackney Wick	Won	42-30
6 August	Home	Belle Vue	Won	37-34
13 August	Home	West Ham	Won	43-28
15 August	Away	Belle Vue	Lost	27-45
19 August	Away	New Cross	Lost	30-42
20 August	Home	Harringay	Won	44-28
27 August	Home	New Cross	Won	47-25
8 September	Away	West Ham	Won	37-34
17 September	Home	New Cross	Won	36-35
19 September	Away	Harringay	Lost	26-45
24 September	Home	Wimbledon	Lost	34-38
24 September	Home	Hackney Wick	Lost	28-44
1 October	Home	Harringay	Won	43-29

National League Table

	Played	Won	Drawn	Lost	For	Against	Points
Belle Vue	24	18	1	5	973	731	37
WEMBLEY	24	15	0	9	891	826	30
Harringay	24	12	0	12	848	868	24
Hackney Wick	24	11	0	13	855	851	22
Wimbledon	24	11	0	13	785	923	22
New Cross	24	9	0	15	844	863	18
West Ham	24	7	1	16	788	922	15

National Trophy

Quarter-Final
Wembley 61 Wimbledon 47
Wimbledon 42 Wembley 65
Aggregate: Wembley 125 Wimbledon 89

Semi-Final
Belle Vue 78 Wembley 30
Wembley 54 Belle Vue 53
Aggregate: Belle Vue 131 Wembley 84

ACU Cup

Pool One
Wembley 54 New Cross 42
Wembley 59 Wimbledon 37
New Cross 37 Wembley 59
Wimbledon 45 Wembley 48
Race Points
Wembley 221
New Cross 178
Wimbledon 174

Final
Belle Vue 51 Wembley 44
Wembley 48 Belle Vue 47
Aggregate: Belle Vue 98 Wembley 92

London Cup

First Round
Wembley: Bye

Semi-Final
Harringay 63 Wembley 44
Wembley 60 Harringay 47
Aggregate: Harringay 110 Wembley 104

TEN

1937 – SECOND AGAIN!

In spite of Jackson's declaration at the end of 1936 that he would only keep three of his riders for 1937, the team he announced as the season started had a familiar ring to it. It was Van Praag (captain), Charles, Lees, Watson, Kilmister, Gregory, Greenwood, Little, Lloyd, Price, Parkinson, Lamont, Millward, Bowden and de la Porte. Over the winter, Lees had changed his mind about retirement. 'I shall ride for another season because my friend, Alec Jackson, needs me,' he told reporters.

Jackson continued to make improvements to the Wembley workshops by acquiring air compressors for rapid and efficient cleaning purposes. The team of mechanics that Jackson had got together spent the winter building a fleet of machines modelled on Charles's mount, as this was considered to be the most reliable in British speedway.

Charles himself had been busy over the winter keeping up his gliding interests. He was still hoping to beat the world's gliding record. It seemed, at this time, to be a perpetual ambition of his that never quite came off.

A new formula was introduced for league racing. Matches would now consist of fourteen heats; each of the team's six best riders would have four races each, while the two reserves would get two races each. This was the first time that reserves were to be given programmed rides in any form of team racing. Cup matches were to retain the eighteen-heat formula but the new rules stated that each team was to consist of eight riders and that 'a team manager may arrange his team as he pleases, subject only to the restriction that no man may ride more than six times nor less than twice.' This also now gave the reserves a minimum of two rides. For the third year running, the same seven teams contested the National League.

Before the season got underway, Jackson decided it would be a good idea if the Lions obtained a real lion as a mascot. With the help of Chapman's Circus in Leicester, he got not one but two nine-month-old lion cubs that he and mechanic Cyril Spinks looked after in the grounds of the Empire Stadium and brought out for publicity purposes as the occasion demanded.

Wembley began their season on Easter Monday, 29 March, with a challenge match at Belle Vue. Although they lost the match by 4 points, Jackson was encouraged by the showing of a number of his riders. Van Praag, Charles and Lees were all in good form, while Kilmister also looked in much better form than the way he had finished the previous season. Even more encouraging was that Price defeated Langton in one outing. So happy was Jackson with the

The 1937 Wembley team. From left to right: Wally Kilmister, Lionel Van Praag, Tommy Price, Cliff Parkinson, Alec Jackson (manager), Frank Charles, Eric Gregory, Ginger Lees, Wally Lloyd.

form of his leading riders that he once again agreed to loan out other members of his team to help lower division clubs. Millward went to Norwich and Bowden and de la Porte to Birmingham Hall Green. He also agreed to transfer Lamont to Hackney Wick for a fee of £300. The only snag here was that Wembley didn't know where he was, as they had had no contact from him over the winter. Nevertheless the deal went through and his whereabouts became Hackney's problem.

As usual, because of the Empire Stadium's other commitments to football and rugby league, Wembley faced a run of five away matches in the league before their first home date. To be able to get in a bit of practice, the Wembley management erected the starting gate in the car park and for over an hour a day Jackson put the team through their paces, practising starts. The area around the starting gate was coated with plenty of cinders, making conditions similar to those on the track itself.

With the riders in good form, their bikes in tip-top condition and their starting technique perfectly honed, the Lions did not expect to have too much difficulty in disposing of Harringay in their first league match on 24 April. The team line-up for this match was Van Praag/Gregory; Little/Kilmister; Charles/Greenwood with Price and Lloyd as reserves. Lees was unfortunately suffering from influenza and could not take part. Charles had recently been in a motor car accident and, although he did take part, was just a shadow of his 1936 self. Van Praag and Gregory dropped just 2 points as a pair, scoring 18 out of a possible 20, but after that, apart from a useful 6 from Lloyd, the rest of the team were hopelessly outclassed and lost by 46 points to 36. The result came like a douche of cold water on the supporters who had been led to believe that this year the Lions would be back where they belonged, at the top. One wrote to the *Speedway News* saying, 'Recently Wembley bought two real lions as mascots for the team. Tell Mr Jackson I have a lovely pair of white mice he can have cheap. They would be far more appropriate at the moment.'

That result was bad enough, but no-one was prepared for what happened to the Lions in their next match as they were massacred 68-16 by the team that had finished bottom of the league in 1936, West Ham. Worse still was the fact that the 1937 team was very little changed from the line-up that had taken the wooden spoon. It is true that Charles missed the match and, although he rode, Lees was still suffering from flu. Nevertheless, there was no excuse for losing thirteen of the fourteen heats 5-1. The only race that did not end in a 5-1 was heat eight and that only

Alec Jackson watches as three of the Lions practise their starts in the car park.

because West Ham's Phil Bishop fell while in second place, leaving Wilkinson to come in first with Lees and Price behind for a 3-3.

From this catastrophe, the worst defeat ever suffered by Wembley, the Lions gradually began to claw their way back. Although they lost their next match away at Belle Vue, it was a much more spirited performance. In fact, it was really only the first two heats that did for them as they lost both 5-1, it briefly looked as though a repeat of the West Ham performance was on the cards. However, they were determined not to let this happen. It was Lees, still fighting against the effects of influenza, who bravely led the fightback when in heat three he startled Kitchen by passing him on the inside to take the race for the Lions. Charles was back in the team and, after a point-less first ride in heat two, he went through the rest of the meeting unbeaten. Greenwood, at reserve, scored 5 paid 6 from his two rides – a reserve's maximum.

Although it was a much better performance, and one that did give a little hope for the future, Jackson was concerned that there was something physically wrong with his team. Lees, he knew, had influenza, but some of the other riders also seemed to lack a bit of verve. Parkinson returned from Australia and as soon as he joined the others for training he too seemed to become ill. Nevertheless, Jackson decided to take a chance on him and put him in the team for the next match against New Cross in place of the even less fit Lees.

Before this match Jackson tried a bit of kidology on the team by telling them that Sir Arthur Elvin himself would be in the stands sizing them all up for the opening home fixture. 'The team [for that match] will be built up on tonight's showing,' he told them. But it was to no avail as once again the team seemed to lack that fighting spirit and lost the match 49-35. Van Praag rode a little better than he had done since the season started for his 8 points, but in general the team had regressed from the Belle Vue encounter.

Suddenly, two nights later, everything changed as the Lions seemed to recover their old spirit and trounced Hackney Wick by 46 points to 38. Van Praag was back on World Championship form with 11 points, while Kilmister made a surprise, but welcome, return to form with 10, even beating Hackney's star rider Cordy Milne in heat eleven. Charles scored 8, losing out to a great piece of team riding between Dick Case and Stan Dell in heat ten. Gregory added 7 while Price, at reserve, scored paid 4 from two rides.

Everything was now set for Wembley's grand reopening on 13 May. The supporters' club once again announced it was well on course to pass the 25,000 mark and a new incentive to join was added. Club members wearing their club badge or flying their car or cycle pennant would be entitled to free admission if spotted by one of the Wembley Supporters' Club scouts outside the stadium. The secretary of the supporters' club was looking forward to the opening meeting of the 1937 season. 'There's nothing quite like a reopening meeting at Wembley,' he said. 'A jolly "how-do-you-do?" atmosphere prevails as friendships and acquaintances that were interrupted by the close of last season are renewed.'

The opening fixture was against New Cross, to whom Wembley had just lost 49-35 away, but the Lions came back with a vengeance, defeating the Rangers, as they had been renamed, by 52 points to 31. Although New Cross supplied the star of the evening in Jack Milne, who went through the card undefeated, it was the all-round performance of the Lions that won the day so convincingly. Van Praag dropped just one point, to Milne. All the rest of the team except Gregory and Lloyd, at reserve, won at least one race. Price once again showed his potential with 5 points from 2 rides, his race with the New Cross captain, Stan Greatrex, in heat eight being the highlight. Greatrex got away from the start first but Price went after him, eventually passing him and winning in fine style. Lees was back in the team, winning two races and showing that he had lost none of his old speed and craft.

The Wembley renaissance continued in their next match away at Wimbledon, where they put on another great display, winning 49-31. Maximums from Van Praag and Charles and 11 points from Kilmister showed that the problems experienced by the team at the beginning of the season were now well and truly behind them. Parkinson followed up his 7 points in the previous fixture with another 7. As well as the general health of the team seeming to be a lot better, many observers put down the win to the gating technique of the Wembley octet. In every race they were off the mark like bullets. That car park training at last looked like paying huge dividends.

Wembley's two leading riders, Charles and Van Praag, were given the honour of captaining their respective countries for the first Test, held at Wembley on 27 May. Van Praag was the better of the two individually, beating Charles in their two outings and scoring 12 points to Charles's 8, but Charles proved to be the more successful captain as England won the match 66-41.

The next league match at the Empire Stadium saw Wembley overcome their old rivals, beating Belle Vue 43-40. Van Praag put in another maximum. For this match, Price was promoted to the team at the expense of Gregory, who was dropped to reserve.

The winning streak continued as, on 17 June, the Lions recorded another narrow victory, this time over Hackney Wick, 44-40. Going into the last heat, the scores were level at 39-39. Out

The programme cover from the first home meeting of the 1937 season, held on 13 May, a National League match against New Cross.

for Wembley were Kilmister and Gregory, back in the team in place of Price, while Hackney tracked Bill Clibbett and George Wilks. As they rounded the first bend, Clibbett took the lead with Gregory in hot pursuit. It continued this way for two-and-a-half laps, when Clibbett's chain went, leaving Gregory and Kilmister to take the 5-1 and the match. Hackney suffered a number of mechanical failures during the match. Wembley, on the other hand, suffered none. It was in close matches like this that the worth of Wembley's mechanical set-up, with their state-of-the-art workshops and top mechanics, really came to the fore.

While the league had been progressing, the first qualifying round of the World Championship had been taking place at other National League tracks, Wembley did not stage one of these because it was allocated the final. Among the twenty-eight qualifiers for the second round were six Wembley riders, Charles, Van Praag, Parkinson, Gregory, Kilmister and Lees.

West Ham were next for Wembley. Still remembering their 68-16 hammering at the start of the season, the Lions were determined to even the score. Eleven points from Van Praag, 10 from Charles, 8 from Lees, 6 from Kilmister and a reserve's maximum from Lloyd ensured that the ghost was laid at last, as Wembley returned the favour, defeating the Hammers by 50 points to 32.

This was the Lions' sixth straight victory. The team had now more or less settled down to Van Praag/Gregory; Charles/Parkinson; Lees/Kilmister with Price and Lloyd at reserve.

Following their poor start to the season, Jackson was very pleased with the way things were now going. From a side thoroughly disorganised by injuries and influenza – at one time or another, Lees, Little, Van Praag, Greenwood and Parkinson had all had the flu or showed flu-like symptoms – the team had ridden their way back into the league reckoning. As well as having a fit team, Jackson put down the improvement to a number of reasons. 'The main factor is harmony,' he said at the time. 'You can have the finest bunch of riders in the world, but if disharmony is apparent points are dropped to inferior riders. Harmony and the Lions go hand in hand. Each rider is out to help the other. You have only to visit our workshops to get proof of that. Each man rides for the team – not newspaper headlines.' Looking to the other reasons why the team was now doing so well, Jackson continued, 'Every Lion will tell you that much of the credit is due to our mechanics. Reliable equipment infuses confidence into a team, and I say without hesitation that no other club possesses more reliable equipment. The mechanics study every minor detail. Nothing but the best will do. A careless mechanic can lose a match. Our staunchest and most loyal supporters are our mechanics.'

Moving on to his junior riders, he revealed perhaps his finest quality as a manager, that of recognising and nurturing talent. 'We have been regarded as fortunate in the fact that Cliff Parkinson, Wally Lloyd and Tommy Price are showing such brilliant form. It's a funny thing, but these folk appear to have overlooked the fact that Wembley has persevered with these three riders. Patience is a great asset in this game – and nowhere else is it exercised so thoroughly as at Wembley. We knew that Parkinson had the riding ability. The trouble was to find an outlet for it. Six months' experimenting during the winter achieved what many folk thought to be impossible. I am not going to divulge that secret – it is locked in our workshops. Wally Lloyd's trouble was starting. We traced the root of the trouble. Now I'm receiving offers for Wally almost each day! But there's nothing doing. Tommy Price, our latest discovery, has the Wembley interests at heart. He is a most conscientious lad, and he has listened to advice. Price is on the up-grade, and when Lees retires – he insists that it is his last season – we hope that our find will step into Ginger's shoes.'

Jackson's determination to support and encourage junior riders led him to announce that in 1938 he would enter a team in the Provincial League made up mostly of young novices, though he also intended to include one or two 'old timers', such as Colin Watson, who would act as 'guides and philosophers' to the youngsters.

By the end of June the Lions had climbed from bottom place in the table to fourth, with 12 points from 10 matches. West Ham were top with 18 points from 12 matches, second were New Cross (18 from 13) and third were Belle Vue with 14 from 12. With their matches in hand, Wembley were back with a chance of taking the league title for the first time since 1932, especially as Belle Vue were not having their usual easy run at the top.

The fight for the league championship was put on the back burner for a while, as Wembley's next encounter was with Second Division Southampton in the quarter-final of the National Trophy. The Provincial League teams had held their own knock-out competition to find one team to enter the quarter-finals alongside the National League teams. Southampton had won the Provincial League final, beating Bristol 93-73 on aggregate. The first leg at Southampton very nearly resulted in the biggest upset in speedway history as the Saints managed to hold Wembley to just a 4-point defeat, going down 40-44. Hero for the home side was Frank Goulden, who scored a maximum 12. Bill Dallison scored 9 from three rides. The tie was held over just fourteen heats and going into heat thirteen the scores were level, but it was a 5-1 in this heat from Charles and Price that finally won the match for Wembley. Southampton declined to race the second leg, which Wembley therefore won on a walkover.

The ACU Cup followed, an away pool match against Wimbledon, which the Lions won comfortably 54-42, Van Praag scoring a maximum and Charles 10.

The last race of the evening, a special race for the top scorers in the cup match, led to some unsavoury scenes as Van Praag and Charles at first refused to race. Five riders had scored 10 or more points in the match, Claude Rye and Eric Collins had scored 11 for the Dons and Wilbur Lamoreaux 10. The steward therefore ordered all five to race. Van Praag and Charles said that it was illegal to include five men in one heat. They were roundly booed and jeered by the home supporters until the steward came down to the track and instructed them to race. The fact that Van Praag then went out and won the race did not go down at all well with some sections of the crowd and, after the meeting, the Wembley riders were surrounded by some angry fans and £3 worth of damage was done to Lees' car. The Wembley management, however, decided not to take the matter any further.

Two more league victories against Harringay, 48-36 (Van Praag and Charles 11 each), and New Cross, 47-36 (Van Praag 11, Charles 10), stretched Wembley's winning sequence in the league to eight matches. Their two leading riders were scoring heavily but there was also solid support from the rest of the team, particularly Gregory and Lees. Lees was no longer the proficient scorer he had been before his injury a couple of seasons ago but he could always be relied upon to put backbone into the middle order. Once again, though, Kilmister was Jackson's real worry. He did not seem to be able to get going and was now the most out-of-touch of the regular team members.

Wembley were now up to third place in the league with 16 points from 12 matches, 2 points behind the leaders West Ham, who had 18 from 12, and second-placed New Cross, who had 18 from 15.

Although they were now back in the race for the league title, Wembley's next two matches put them out of the National Trophy as, on successive days, 14 and 15 July, they were beaten home and away by New Cross. The first, at the Old Kent Road track, saw them lose by 59 points to 48. Van Praag was once again on top form, losing just once to Jack Milne. Charles registered 12 while Lees added 10. With just 11 points in it, there was a reasonable expectation from the Lions' supporters that their team would go through to the final, especially in view of their recent league form. But it was not to be. Wembley were virtually a two-man team as Van Praag went through the meeting unbeaten and Charles added 15. Lees was next highest with 8. Far from pulling back the 11-point deficit, Wembley actually lost on their home track 58-50, going down 117-98 on aggregate.

In the ACU Cup match the following week against Harringay, the Lions looked a different team. There was much more determination about their riding and it was a much happier Jackson who saw his team win 53-42. It almost went without saying at the time that Van Praag scored another home maximum. Charles added 10 paid 11 and Lees 9 paid 10. What was most heartening to Jackson, however, was the fact that Kilmister rode more like the Kilmister of old, scoring 8 points from 3 races. There was one drawback to the evening, however, and that was an injury to Gregory, who was later found to have broken his collarbone in a fall. Lloyd was moved up to the team from reserve to take his place. Returning to the team at reserve came Colin Watson for his first team outing since breaking his leg on Good Friday 1935.

The following night something had to give as Wembley found themselves at Waterden Road in the league. Wembley had so far chalked up a sequence of eight consecutive victories in the league, whereas Hackney Wick had also won their last eight home matches in the league. With maximums from Van Praag and Charles and 11 points from Lees, it was the Lions who maintained their record, beating Hackney 49-34. Watson managed 1 point when, in heat eight, Cordy Milne's bike packed up and he came in third. This win moved Wembley up to joint first in the league, equal on points with West Ham, having raced two more fixtures overall but one less at home. It promised to be a close finish to the season as both New Cross and Belle Vue were breathing down their necks, just two points behind. Wembley's next match would be crucial to their hopes of regaining the title, as it was away at West Ham.

But before that could take place, the Lions had another ACU Cup match against Harringay, which they won comfortably 51-33. All four of the leading Lions scored well – Van Praag yet another maximum, Lees 10, Charles 9 and Kilmister 8. The return to top form of both Lees and Kilmister augured well for the league battles to come. In fact, Lees was so pleased with his form that he hinted he may not make his annual retirement announcement at the end of the season!

The vital match against West Ham started fairly evenly. Van Praag, Charles, Lees and Kilmister were all riding well. Van Praag won his first two heats, beating both the Hammers' stars, Wilkinson and Stevenson, and setting a new track record in heat one. But there was a disaster in heat nine. When the two-minute warning sounded none of the riders were ready to come to the tapes. With just thirty seconds to go, the two West Ham riders, Eric Chitty and Arthur Atkinson, made their way to the tapes, but there was no sign of the two Wembley boys, Van Praag and Lloyd. Just as the two minutes were up they both came hurrying out of the pits but it was too late; their exclusion lights were on. They were replaced by reserves Little and Price and, although Price rode well to defeat Atkinson for second place, West Ham scored a 4-2 and went on to take the match 49-34. For some reason the double exclusion seemed to have a very unsettling effect on the team and they lost two of the last four heats by 5-1 and one by 4-2. In modern football parlance, this match was a 'four-pointer', and Wembley's first loss in ten league matches was a big blow to their title hopes, though not yet a knock-out.

Their hopes of taking at least one trophy remained alive, however, as they beat New Cross away 48-47 in the ACU Cup. Once again Van Praag picked up a maximum and received brilliant support from a revitalised Lees, who scored 11, and Charles, with 10. The following evening they completed the double over New Cross, beating them 54.5-41.5 at the Empire Stadium. For once Van Praag failed to score a maximum as he fell in heat eight. The fact that he fell while in the lead meant that the race became much more exciting than it might otherwise have been. As they swerved to avoid him, Lloyd and the Rangers' Stan Greatrex found themselves racing shoulder to shoulder. From then on the race became one of the best seen at Wembley that season as first one then the other managed to get a few inches' lead on his opponent. Coming out of the last bend, Lloyd was just a shade ahead but, with the crowd shouting itself hoarse, Greatrex moved up to the Lion and they hurled themselves across the line together to chalk up a dead heat. The noise from this heat had scarcely died down when the riders in the following heat almost repeated the feat. This time the race was between Lees and New Cross's American star Jack Milne. As before, it was the New Cross rider who had to catch up along the home straight. As they hurtled across the line, the crowd thought it was another dead heat but the steward just managed to separate them, awarding the race to Milne. This was Lees' only defeat of the night, while Charles turned in a maximum. Van Praag won his other three races. Price, promoted to the team for the evening, scored his highest score so far for the Lions with 8 points. Watson, at reserve, managed another point.

For the second half, Jackson laid on midget car racing, which was becoming a very popular attraction at a number of speedway tracks around the country. Unfortunately it did not have the same appeal at Wembley. It was very noticeable that immediately the speedway finished thousands left the stadium. According to the *Speedway News* reporter they didn't miss much. 'The midgets didn't cause a single cheer,' he wrote. 'Three cars in one race sounded promising, but they went into the first bend, one, two, three, and finished in the same order so there wasn't anything to shout about at all.'

Wembley progressed to the semi-final of the London Cup, defeating Harringay 58-49 at home and 61-46 away. Both Van Praag and Charles scored maximums in the home leg. In the away leg, inevitably, Van Praag scored another maximum while Charles lost just once to record 17, and Lees contributed 16.

Wembley's hopes of taking the league title received a boost when, in another 'four-pointer', Wembley overcame West Ham at home by 44 points to 40. To strengthen the team Jackson had signed up former Stamford Bridge and Wimbledon favourite Gus Kuhn, who made his debut for the Lions in this match. Once again, victory was assured by maximums from Van Praag and Charles, while Price turned in another creditable score with 7. Kuhn managed one point from his two rides.

At the end of August, West Ham still led the table with 32 points from Wembley on 24. But crucially, the Lions now had five matches in hand over the Hammers, so a win in all of them would see Wembley on top. The destiny of the 1937 National League title was now in their own hands.

They also had high hopes of the ACU Cup as they made it through to the final following a 58-38 defeat of Wimbledon. It is probably unnecessary to say that Van Praag and Charles both scored maximums. Lees added 8 from three races while Price, now fast moving up to heat-leader standard, contributed 9.

The following Wednesday Wembley, in desperate need of a league win, went down by just one point away at New Cross, 42-41. A poor night for Charles was probably what did for the Lions. He won two races but came last in two. Van Praag scored 11 points but it wasn't enough.

The next night, the 1937 World Championship final was held at the Empire Stadium in front of yet another record crowd of 85,000. The same three Wembley riders as had qualified for the 1936 final also qualified for the 1937 final, Van Praag, Charles and Lees. The bonus points system remained. Jack Milne had the most bonus points with 13. Van Praag had 11 while Charles and Lees had 10 each. Given his recent devastating form in the league, Van Praag was one of the favourites to retain his title. The other leading favourites were the three Americans, Jack and Cordy Milne and Wilbur Lamoreaux, and the man Van Praag had beaten in the run-off last year, Eric Langton. The 1936 maximum man, Bluey Wilkinson, had unfortunately injured a wrist earlier in the season and had not been able to qualify.

It was not to be Van Praag's night as he was plagued by mechanical trouble, not finishing one heat, coming last in another and not even starting in one. He won the other two heats, which may give some indication of how he might have done. Before the meeting started it was reported that he had spent fifteen hours a day for the last month with his mechanic making sure his bike was perfect for the big night. Charles fared little better, coming last in his first two races and third in his third, before finding his form and winning his last two races. Van Praag and Charles finished equal sixth overall. Surprisingly, the top Wembley rider was Lees, who had a steady if unspectacular evening, although he was involved in the best heat of the night when he and Kitchen battled it out over all four laps, with the Lion just taking it on the line. He finished with an overall 19 points to finish one place above his colleagues in fifth. This year there was no controversy over the bonus points as Jack Milne scored a maximum 15 points to go with his 13 bonus points to take the title. The three Americans swept the board, taking first, second and third with Jack Milne, Lamoreaux and Cordy Milne in that order.

Back to league racing the following week, Wembley had an easy win over Wimbledon. The expected maximum from Van Praag was supported by 11 points from Lees, continuing his good run-in to the end of the season.

The following week saw another fine win for the Lions as they beat Belle Vue 50-34. It is true that Belle Vue were not the force they had been the previous three seasons, but nevertheless it was a convincing win over a team that included riders of the calibre of Langton, Varey, Abbott and Kitchen. Van Praag's inevitable maximum was backed up by 11 from Charles and 8 from Lees. Gregory returned to the side following his injury, taking the place of Kuhn at reserve.

In spite of the form of their three heat leaders, Wembley finally lost their chance of pulling off the league title two nights later on 18 September, as they went down by just 2 points at Green Lanes to Harringay. With one heat to go, the scores were level. For this heat, on which the whole of the season's National League competition hinged, the Lions were represented by Price and Gregory, while Harringay had Bill Pitcher and Les Wotton. In truth it was not much of a race as Wotton won from the start and behind him there was a procession consisting of Gregory, Pitcher and Price, in that order, a 4-2 for Harringay and Wembley's hopes dashed.

Wembley finished their league season at home with easy victories over Wimbledon, 55-28, and Harringay, 53-28, Lees scoring 12 and 11 respectively. Although their very last match of the season ended in a 52-31 defeat away to Belle Vue they were by then assured of the runners up spot for the second year running and the third time in four years. It was their away form that had let them down as they did not lose one league match at home in 1937.

Van Praag's points return in the league had been nothing short of phenomenal towards the end of the season. Between 7 May and 30 September he had taken eighteen double-figure hauls out of a possible nineteen. The only one he missed was when he took just three rides at West Ham on 27 July, winning them all. He finished the season with six consecutive full maximums at home.

In the overall League averages he finished in second place with a cma of 10.53 behind Jack Milne, who had a staggering 11.09. Charles finished in tenth place with 8.96, while Lees' late run gave him a cma of 8.24. Price had performed exceptionally well in his first full year of senior racing, ending the year with an average of 5.48.

However, there were still two cups for Wembley to compete in, the ACU Cup and the London Cup. First up was the London Cup semi-final, which turned out to be a repeat of the National Trophy semi-final as they were bundled out by New Cross, the Rangers winning both legs, 56-50 at the Empire Stadium and 62-46 on their own track. Their one last chance of a trophy came with the ACU Cup final, in which they were up against Belle Vue. The first leg, at the Empire Stadium, resulted in a narrow victory for the Lions by 49 points to 45. Van Praag got his usual maximum, Charles scored 10, Kilmister 9 and Gregory 8. But four points seemed hardly enough to take back to Hyde Road and so it proved as the Aces laid about the hapless Lions, beating them 61-35. Wembley's season finished with no silverware to put in their trophy cupboard. They were runners-up in the National League and the ACU Cup and semi-finalists in the National Trophy and the London Cup.

At the end of the season the Wembley captain Van Praag reflected on what might have been. He said he wasn't too downhearted and he reminded everyone of how the Lions had started the season with four straight defeats due to their influenza epidemic. If they had been able to put out a full team and won just two of those matches, the league title would have been theirs. He went on to say that 'We are a very happy family at Wembley and my teammates have, at all times, tried their utmost. We all get "off days" of course, but the team's riding as a whole has more than encouraged the belief that next year will be our year. Young Tommy Price has come on splendidly, and a winter's rest will work wonders for him. He has acquired that confidence in himself and is not now susceptible to failures. Worry is worse than a bare track to a rider! Cliff Parkinson has shown that he is a tactical rider, and his steady performances are much appreciated by the rest of the lads. As the same team is being retained for next season I see no reason why one or more trophies should not find their way Wembley-wards. We are all confident of doing well in 1938 – a confidence that is based on real facts, and not on mere optimism.'

Van Praag himself had a very happy to end to the season as, on 1 October at Hendon Registry Office, he married his long-time fiancée, Miss Gwen Hipkin.

1937 National League Averages – qualification 6 matches

	Matches	Rides	Points	BP	Total	CMA
Lionel Van Praag	24	95	250	0	250	10.53
Frank Charles	23	92	202	4	206	8.96
Ginger Lees	21	83	165	6	171	8.24
Eric Gregory	17	65	82	19	101	6.22
Wally Kilmister	24	90	105	21	126	5.60
Tommy Price	24	73	80	20	100	5.48
Cliff Parkinson	20	73	78	18	96	5.26
Wally Lloyd	24	67	69	16	85	5.07
Gus Kuhn	6	12	11	3	14	4.67

National League Matches

Date	H/A	Against	W/L/D	Score
24 April	Away	Harringay	Lost	36-46
27 April	Away	West Ham	Lost	16-68
1 May	Away	Belle Vue	Lost	36-48
5 May	Away	New Cross	Lost	35-49
7 May	Away	Hackney Wick	Won	46-38
13 May	Home	New Cross	Won	52-31
17 May	Away	Wimbledon	Won	49-31
3 June	Home	Belle Vue	Won	43-40
17 June	Home	Hackney Wick	Won	44-40
24 June	Home	West Ham	Won	52-30
1 July	Home	Harringay	Won	48-36
8 July	Home	New Cross	Won	47-36
23 July	Away	Hackney Wick	Won	49-34
27 July	Away	West Ham	Lost	34-49
2 August	Away	Wimbledon	Won	51-33
19 August	Home	West Ham	Won	44-40
28 August	Home	Hackney Wick	Won	45-39
1 September	Away	New Cross	Lost	41-42
9 September	Home	Wimbledon	Won	56-28
16 September	Home	Belle Vue	Won	50-34
18 September	Away	Harringay	Lost	41-43
25 September	Home	Wimbledon	Won	55-28
30 September	Home	Harringay	Won	53-28
2 October	Away	Belle Vue	Lost	31-52

National League Table

	Played	Won	Drawn	Lost	For	Against	Points
West Ham	24	18	0	6	1,129	859	36
WEMBLEY	24	16	0	8	1,054	943	32
New Cross	24	16	0	8	1,042.5	957.5	32
Belle Vue	24	13	0	11	1,094	909	26
Hackney Wick	24	10	0	14	935.5	1,062.5	20
Harringay	24	9	0	15	929	1,064	18
Wimbledon	24	2	0	22	799	1,188	4

National Trophy

Quarter-Final
Southampton 40 Wembley 44
Wembley: Walkover
Aggregate: Wembley 44 Southampton 40

Semi-Final
New Cross 59 Wembley 48
Wembley 50 New Cross 58
Aggregate: New Cross 117 Wembley 98

ACU Cup

Pool Two
Wembley 53 Harringay 42
Wembley 54.5 New Cross 41.5
Wembley 58 Wimbledon 38
Harringay 44 Wembley 52
New Cross 47 Wembley 48
Wimbledon 42 Wembley 54

Race Points
Wembley 319.5
New Cross 311.5
Harringay 269
Wimbledon 240

Final
Belle Vue 61 Wembley 35
Wembley 49 Belle Vue 45
Aggregate: Belle Vue 106 Wembley 84

London Cup

First Round
Wembley 58 Harringay 49
Harringay 46 Wembley 61
Aggregate: Wembley 119 Harringay 95

Semi-Final
New Cross 62 Wembley 46
Wembley 50 New Cross 56
Aggregate: New Cross 118 Wembley 96

NO. 5 – LIONEL VAN PRAAG

Lionel Van Praag was born in Sydney on 17 December 1908. By the age of fifteen he was proficient in a number of sports, especially boxing and rugby, and was chosen to represent New South Wales at rugby league. To facilitate transport to the rugby matches his father bought him a 750cc Indian. Apart from going to rugby he used it to visit places he'd not been able to get to before. One such place was the Sydney speedway track, promoted by Johnnie Hoskins. He became engrossed in the sport and an ardent spectator, before deciding he wanted to have a go himself.

Van Praag later talked about what it was that made him take up speedway, 'I always had the urge to take things apart to see what made them go. This urge led me to my first job when I left school, working in a typewriter factory repairing machines. This job provided the necessary funds for me to take in some of the entertainments about the town – one of which was speedway racing, then an attraction in Sydney. As I sat and watched the riders whirling round the circuit I thought that here was an excellent opportunity of making a good living – and having some grand fun at the same time – so then and there I made up my mind to see what was in store for me in this sport. I shall always be grateful to Johnnie Hoskins, for it was he who gave me my first trial on the cinders – and it certainly proved to be a lucky break.'

By the end of the 1926 season he was beginning to enjoy a certain amount of success at Hoskins' Sydney Showground circuit and his exploits came to the attention of the Brisbane promoter A.J. Hunting, who signed him on for the following season. At Brisbane he found himself in the company of some of the top stars of the day including Vic Huxley, Dicky Smythe, Frank Pearce and Charlie Spinks. This high class of opposition helped his own riding improve and by 1928 he had reached a good standard.

When speedway started in Britain in 1928, Hunting brought his top riders over to show the British what real speedway was all about. Van Praag turned down the opportunity, deciding to stay at home instead, travelling round various tracks. It was not until 1931 that he took the plunge and came over, immediately linking up with Wembley. He later explained why this was: 'Believe it or not the English climate had a lot to do with my tardy arrival in this country – that and a Depression – that was always a chief grumble on the riders' return to Australia. For three whole years I shirked coming to England, where a combination of bad weather and poor business seemed to be the only reward for speedway riders, until one day I was attracted

Lionel Van Praag.

by a sudden splurge of shiny new cars, smart clothes and a general air of prosperity among the lads. Then and there I made up my mind to "suffer" in this unwelcome climate and supposed Depression that, according to my rivals, was the constant lot of those living in England.'

It took him a few years to find his feet with Wembley and it wasn't until his appointment as team captain in 1935 that he finally showed the form that had made him such a top-class rider in Australia. Taking his responsibilities very seriously, the appointment seemed to transform him. Until then he had been known as something of a practical joker. One of his more famous exploits, for example, was holding up a bank in Australia with a toy pistol. After he became captain, the *Speedway News* reported a conversation between two of the sport's pioneers discussing Van Praag. One of them said, 'I can hardly believe he is the same man. I don't believe butter would melt in his mouth, but do you remember…'

His new responsible outlook on life meant that he trained properly and looked after his machinery properly. The result was not only good for the team but good for himself as during 1936 he became one of speedway's top riders, scoring four full league maximums on the trot between 27 June and 31 July, including three on away tracks. The 1936 season culminated with him being crowned speedway's first World Champion.

His amazing league form continued for the next three seasons, as he averaged 10.53, 10.50 and 10.61. He also qualified for the three remaining pre-war World finals, finishing sixth and fourth in 1937 and 1938 respectively – the 1939 final being abandoned because of the Second World War.

His new approach to speedway from 1935 onwards also saw him appointed Australian Test captain. Altogether he rode in 36 Tests, scoring 297 points.

During the Second World War he was awarded the George Medal for saving the life of a colleague after their plane had been shot down over the Timor Sea. Carrying his unconscious partner, Van Praag had swum for thirty hours through shark-infested waters before finding land.

He returned for one further season after the Second World War in 1947 when he rode for New Cross and qualified for the British Riders' Championship final. His last Test series was in 1950/51 in Australia.

ELEVEN

1938 – NEW BLOOD

Wembley's first act of 1938 was to sign up two teenage juniors, Jeff Lloyd, brother of Wally Lloyd, and Sam Warren. It was a sign of what was to come in 1938 as Jackson looked to rebuild his team following the retirement of Lees, the realisation that Watson was never going to make it back into the line-up and the announcement by Kilmister that he may not always be available because of his business commitments. In a somewhat curious move he also signed up Australian pioneer Frank Arthur, after being assured that he was showing a 'rare turn of speed' back in his native Australia. Dicky Case was signed up in place of Wally Little, who moved to Wimbledon. Case ran a successful training school at Rye House and Jackson wanted his expertise to help him in his mission of finding and bringing on junior talent. Two other juniors were taken on: George Wilks, transferred from Hackney Wick for £350, and Malcolm Craven, a product of Arthur Warwick's training school at Dagenham, where he had equalled Frank Hodgson's track record in his first outing. Craven had graduated to speedway from road racing at Donington. He first tried his luck on the oval circuits at Barnet and in his first meeting he finished third in the final of the South Midland Championship. He started visiting Wembley to see how the 'big boys' did it and was soon acting as general help, support and bag carrier to his idol, Colin Watson. It was Watson who advised him to place himself in the expert hands of Arthur Warwick and then advised Jackson that here was a youngster worth taking a chance on.

News of Jackson's search for new young riders spread fast round the speedway world and even before the season started he had turned down over 200 applications.

The National League once again comprised seven teams, but there was a change to the tracks involved as Bristol replaced Hackney Wick, who dropped down to the Second Division. A new competition was introduced – the English Trophy. This was for Second Division teams and First Division reserve teams and was split into Southern and Northern Sections, the winners of each meeting for the trophy. Wembley Reserves were in the Southern Section along with Birmingham, Hackney Wick, Norwich, Southampton and New Cross Reserves.

The first meeting of the 1938 season, an individual trophy called the Opening Cup, took place at New Cross on 3 April. The Wembley contingent, consisting of Gregory, Price, Wilks and Craven, did well, with Price and Gregory finishing second and third behind West Ham's Eric Chitty. Considering none of these riders were heat leaders and they were up against the likes of Chitty, Langton, George Newton, Stan Greatrex and Tommy Croombs, things augured

Malcolm Craven.

well for the Lions. Once again, much of their success was put down to their finely tuned motors that, as always, had been expertly prepared by the Wembley mechanics in the Wembley workshops.

Hackney Wick also held an individual trophy for their opening meeting. In a stunning performance, Wembley junior Malcolm Craven carried all before him, scoring a maximum 15 points and winning the final to take the All Star Gold Cup. It was yet further proof that the Wembley juniors were ready to step into the shoes of their senior colleagues and raised the Lions' hopes of ending the season with some silverware. Still hoping to make his comeback to the big time, Watson appeared in this meeting, scoring 9 points.

Just as the league racing season was about to start, a question arose as to whether Arthur would be allowed to ride for Wembley after all. Harringay, who still had him on their retained list, began to waver over their intention to transfer him. As discussions went on between the two clubs, there were reports from Australia that Arthur had decided against coming over to England, so the whole thing was academic anyway. Jackson assured the Lions' supporters that Arthur would definitely be riding for Wembley this year but, in the event, it turned out not to be the case.

Wembley's first match of the season as a team was a friendly away to West Ham. The chosen team consisted of Van Praag/Gregor; Case/Price; Charles/Wilks with Kilmister and Craven at reserve. It was a new-look team compared to the one that had finished the previous season but one thing remained the same – Van Praag scored a maximum. However, he was the only one to show to any advantage, as all the pre-season hopes of the new young Wembley squad crumbled into the Custom House dust. Apart from Van Praag it was a poor performance as the Lions went down 56-28.

Things started to look up, however, when they took on and beat newcomers Bristol in their first league match of the season. Continuing his incredible run, Van Praag scored yet another maximum, with Charles adding 11. Even better from the Lions' point of view was the fact that Wilks scored 9 points and Craven won one of his reserve races, beating a young Australian by the name of Vic Duggan. The final score was Bristol 37 Wembley 47.

A couple of days later the second team was out in an English Trophy match away to Southampton. The team for this was a mixture of youth and experience, with the line-up being Watson/Kuhn; Craven/Andy Menzies; Parkinson/Jeff Lloyd and Bowden and Kaines at reserve. Only Craven put up any serious challenge to the Saints, scoring 9 points in a 53-29 defeat.

For their next match against the New Cross Reserves, Kuhn was dropped to make way for Gregory and Price came in for Craven. Watson, for the first time, began to look something like his old self as he rattled off 10 paid 11. Price also scored 10 points as the Wembley Reserves won by 49 points to 34.

The first team did not fare so well on their trip to New Cross, going down 45-39. Van Praag missed out on his customary maximum, scoring a mere 11 after losing to the World Champion Jack Milne on his own track in the opening heat. Wilks was once again very impressive and was second top scorer with 7 after failing to score in his first outing.

Wembley's next match was against Belle Vue on 12 May and was their first home fixture of the season. Some alterations had been made to the track, which had been slightly banked to the extent of eight inches. Jackson explained, 'We had a few meetings washed out through flooding last season and the only way to ensure a trouble-free time this year was to tear the surface right up, install a better drainage system and build up the track from the fence so that the water can drain to the inner edge and be carried away.' Other changes at the Empire Stadium included moving the steward's rostrum from inside the track to high up in the roof. This was a welcome move to those fans who stood or sat on the back straight, as the rostrum had hidden the start and finish line from their view. Also, the formerly sparse Press gallery was turned into a more upmarket club-cum-bar for wining and dining the Press, and a new indicator board used to give results for the greyhound racing and the speedway was built.

During the winter Jackson and Van Praag had been working on a new tyre, which Jackson hoped would be ready for the opening meeting at the Empire Stadium. It was being manufactured by Dunlop and designed to give quick starting and grip on the bends. The design had wider spaced studs than was normal so as to avoid clogging, with a thickness of intermediate rubber that allowed deeper and more frequent grinding than other tyres then in use.

The opening match turned into a very one-sided affair as Belle Vue turned up without Langton, and Varey was out of the meeting after just a quarter of a lap when he crashed into the fence in the opening heat. Nevertheless, Wembley did what they had to do, winning the match convincingly 54-30, with Van Praag scoring his usual maximum. But even more encouraging for the Lions was the fact that Wilks also scored a full maximum. In the second half both Jack Milne and Wilbur Lamoreaux broke Frank Charles' existing 18-second Cinders Record with times of 17.6 seconds and 17.4 seconds respectively.

With Varey back in action for the return at Belle Vue two days later, Wembley did not have such an easy time of it, as Varey's maximum helped the Aces to a 48-36 win. Van Praag scored 10 but his only real support came from Charles with 8. The regular team was now more or less settled as Van Praag/Gregory; Charles/Price; Case/Wilks with Kilmister and Craven as reserves.

It was an interesting mix of youth and experience that Jackson hoped would not only pay full dividends in the current season but would lay the foundations for a championship team of the future.

The next match away at West Ham saw much the same pattern of scoring for the team as Van Praag and Charles both scored 10, with the next highest being 4 from Gregory and Craven as the Lions went down 40-34. The track was very slippery due to rain and in heat eleven Wilks fell. Case and West Ham's Canadian star Jimmy Gibb were following close behind but both just managed to lay down their machines to avoid him. Because the track was so wet, both riders and bikes slid along the ground, with Case being thrown onto Wilks' still-spinning machine. He suffered severe bruising as a result and was put out of action for some time.

Parkinson was brought in to replace him for the return match at Wembley two days later, with Kilmister moving back up into the team proper. Parkinson took his opportunity well, scoring 8 points, and with Van Praag's maximum, 9 from Charles and 7 from Wilks, the Lions came out as winners 44-40.

Wembley's next match at Wimbledon had one of the most exciting finishes of the season. Because of his showing at the Empire Stadium, Parkinson was promoted to the team proper with Price dropping down to reserve. With one heat to go the scores were level. Nobby Key and former Lion Norman Evans were out for Wimbledon in the last heat, while the Lions had Gregory and Wilks as their pair. Evans and Key got out of the gate first, with Gregory in hot pursuit. Gregory had so far managed only two points all night, while Wilks, unusually for him, had failed to score at all. It looked like being a narrow win for the Dons. But Gregory did not give up. Passing Key, he set out in pursuit of Evans, gradually eating into his lead, until by the final bend he was just inches behind. In a do-or-die effort round the outside, Gregory just managed to pass his rival, maintaining his lead to the finishing line, and turning a win for Wimbledon into a 42-42 draw.

The return match at the Empire Stadium three days later was another close-run affair. This time the Lions held a two-point lead going in to the final heat. With the exception of Eric Collins taking the place of Nobby Key, the same riders were involved. This time, however, the hero of Plough Lane, Gregory, was excluded for crossing the white line and it was left to Wilks to take the points for Wembley, which he did quite easily to ensure the victory 43-41. His total score on the night was 10, two behind his captain's maximum.

Kilmister was not having a good season and was just a shadow of the rider of former days. He decided that a small change of style was the answer. He had always been a bit of a do-or-die merchant but he now decided to take this to even greater extremes and model himself on Billy Lamont, risking all on the outside line. In the match against Wimbledon, therefore, he flew round the boards, taking the bends as fast as he could, scraping the fence as he went. It was very spectacular for the crowd, but it did not help his points total as, once again, he could only manage 2.

Van Praag had been injured in the second half of the Wembley match and missed the next home match, with the result that Wembley went down at home in the league for the first time since September 1936. The lucky team to meet the Lions without their captain was New Cross. Watson was brought into the team at reserve, while Price moved back into the team proper. In Van Praag's absence, Wilks was top scorer with 8, one more than Charles and Parkinson. The final score was Wembley 37 New Cross 46.

Still without their captain and top scorer, Wembley then pulled off an amazing away win at Harringay, largely thanks to Charles and Wilks, who scored 11 and 10 respectively. Once again there was good support from Parkinson, who turned in 6 in the 45-38 victory.

With Test matches, cup matches and World Championship rounds taking place, league racing took a back seat for a while after this match. At this time Wembley were lying in fourth place in the league with 11 points from 10 matches. At the head of the table were New Cross with 16 from 11. Although there were many more matches to go before the season was over, it was already apparent that New Cross were the team to beat and Wembley were slipping behind.

Next up at the Empire Stadium was the second Test. Australia had won the first Test 56-52 at Belle Vue. This time it was England's turn to come out on top, 63-44. Back from his injury, the Wembley and Australian captain Van Praag rode magnificently for his team, scoring 15 points, the same as Wilkinson, accounting for almost three-quarters of the Australian total. Charles, appointed England captain for the night, did not do quite so well, but still managed 13 points.

A thunderstorm with torrential rain greeted the Lions on their visit to Bristol to race their first ACU Cup match of the season. Fortunately, the weather cleared about half an hour before the meeting was due to begin, but the rain had left the track very greasy and it was the Wembley riders who got to grips with the conditions quicker. Charles and Van Praag once again put on virtuoso performances, scoring 13 paid 14 and 12 paid 13 respectively, while Parkinson and Wilks also rode as if there were no problem with the track, scoring 10 and 8. Even Kilmister at reserve had his best meeting for a long time, taking a reserve's paid maximum with 5 paid 6. The only real opposition was Cordy Milne, who scored 17, being beaten just once by Charles in the last heat. The final score was Bristol 44 Wembley 64.

Wembley's next ACU Cup pool match was against Wimbledon at Plough Lane. As in their last two encounters, this one too was very close, Wimbledon winning by a single point 54-53. The most encouraging aspect for Wembley was the good form shown by Kilmister, whose score of 11 paid 12 included three race wins.

Wembley's return ACU Cup encounter with Bristol at the Empire Stadium proved to be a little easier as they ran out winners 61-47. This time the Lions' hero was Price, who rattled off four straight wins in his first four races and finished as top scorer with 14, equal to Van Praag. Heat eight proved to be a curious heat as, right at the start, the Wembley captain, in the red helmet and drawn on the inside, wobbled and crossed onto the grass. His red disqualification light went on immediately, but he didn't see it. As the riders came round for the second lap, the marshal waved a black flag and a red flag, meaning that the rider in red is excluded and should stop racing. But instead of that happening, all four riders stopped wondering what the red flag was for. It was Bristol's Danish rider, Morian Hansen, who first realised what was happening and promptly started racing again. His partner, Milne, and Wilks followed shortly after but Hansen won the race with half a lap to spare amid a sustained outburst of booing. The steward, quite rightly, gave the result as first Hansen, second Milne, third Wilks. The Wembley announcer said, 'We accept the verdict in true Wembley sporting fashion.' Obviously not!

There was a complete change in fortunes in the two pool matches against Belle Vue. In London, Wembley beat Belle Vue 67-40; back in Manchester the Aces thrashed the Lions 71-36. Charles, who was suffering from a poisoned knee, did not ride in either match. In the home tie, the tall Australian junior Andy Menzies made his first-team debut at reserve while Craven moved up into the team. Menzies retained his place at Belle Vue. Kilmister was dropped and Bowden brought into the team.

Although the score in the second match looked bad, Wembley suffered a number of injuries during the match. In heat two Wilks fell and was not able to compete properly after that. In heat ten Craven collided with Belle Vue's Walter Hull and fell awkwardly. He took no further part in the meeting after he was diagnosed as suffering from concussion and Van Praag suffered from a badly cut ankle. All this left Gregory as top scorer for the Lions with 10 points.

The Wembley pair of Van Praag and Gregory were the Lions' entrants in the first official Team Pairs Championship held at New Cross on 22 June. That they finished the evening as joint winners was largely due to Van Praag, who scored a fifteen-point maximum out of their total score of 21. Harringay, in the shape of Les Wotton and Alec Statham, shared the trophy.

Van Praag led Australia again in the third Test at New Cross, this time scoring a magnificent 18-point maximum to lead his team to a 61-47 victory. In contrast, Charles had a very poor meeting, failing to score any points at all.

Having tried the 'Billy Lamont' solution to his problem of loss of form, Kilmister now came up with another answer. 'I need an evening at Wimbledon to set me going,' he said. 'It's a track which just inspires me; I feel right on top there. Why Wimbledon? Goodness only knows – it's no easier than many other circuits, but it gives me the right hunch and when I've got it, it stays for a while. If it begins to fade… well, all I ask is for another dose of Wimbledon!'

On the last day of June Wembley were back in league action, taking on Harringay at home. Charles was still unfit to ride but Case was back in the line-up. In a good all-round performance, the Lions trounced the Tigers by 50 points to 34. Van Praag won all his races for 12 points, but behind him there was a solid performance from the rest of the team as Case scored 8, Price 7, Wilks 6, Craven 6 and Gregory 5. Even the two reserves did well, with Kilmister scoring 3 paid 5 from two rides and Craven 3, also from two.

It was the sort of team performance Wembley needed if they were to put in a challenge for the league title. And with Charles due back soon, things were looking good. A lot of this was due to the youngsters, such as Price, Wilks and Craven, that Jackson had been nurturing. There was much muttering at the time that Jackson was 'lucky' in having found three outstanding juniors to take the place of the likes of Lees and Watson, but the truth of the matter was that it was not luck at all. Jackson could spot the best and then once he had found them he knew exactly what to do to get the best out of them. As an expert mechanic himself, he also made sure his youngsters had the best possible equipment. Price, Wilks and Craven had all started at other tracks and had been let go because their managers had neither the skill nor perseverance to do what Jackson had done. He now announced that he had found another in the same mould, Bob Wells. After just one second-half reserves race at Wembley, which he won, beating Watson among others, he was put into the reserves team, scoring 8 points on his debut at Hackney.

Wembley's next two meetings were the home and away legs of the National Trophy first round. They had been drawn against the team that had defeated them in two previous finals, Belle Vue, and they were out for revenge. Van Praag, with a paid maximum, and Charles, with 15 points, were the main architects of the first leg 61-47 home victory, but Price and Craven also played their parts with 7 and 6. But would a fourteen-point lead be enough to take to Manchester?

After the first two heats, it looked as though it would be as Van Praag and Price scored a 4-2 in the opening race and Wilks and Charles a 5-1 in the second, extending the lead to 20 points.

Tommy Price.

But the Aces gradually came back at them and after heat thirteen the Lions' lead had been cut to six points. Reserves Case and Kilmister came out in heat fourteen to score a very welcome 5-1, but Belle Vue returned the favour in the next heat. But with just three heats to go time was running out for the Aces. A 3-3 in the next heat, thanks to Price and Wilks taking second and third places, meant that Wembley needed just four points from the last two heats to make sure of victory, and with Case and Craven also packing second and third for three in the penultimate heat, it just needed one of the Wembley riders to finish in the final heat. It was a 5-1 to Belle Vue, but it didn't matter. On the night Belle Vue won 60-48, but the overall aggregate showed the narrowest of victories for the Lions, 109-107. Wembley had, at last, laid their National Trophy bogey team to rest. Price was top scorer for Wembley with 12 points.

After their three close encounters earlier in the season, the Wembley/Wimbledon ACU Cup match turned into yet another last-heat decider, with the scores level going into heat eighteen. Out for Wimbledon were Geoff Pymar and Wilbur Lamoreaux, while Wembley went with Van Praag and Parkinson. Unfortunately, after an evening of close, exciting racing, this crucial race turned out to be the most boring of them all as Van Praag shot away from the start and never looked like being headed while Parkinson fell, so the result was a 3-3 and another tied match, 54-54.

By this time, both Jackson and Watson realised that he was never going to get back to the form that had made him a regular choice for Wembley, and so Jackson allowed him to try his hand with West Ham, for whom he rode in a number of reserve matches. Although only on loan for the rest of the season, it was essentially the end at Wembley for one of the Lions' greatest riders and one of their most loyal servants.

The first round of the World Championship had now finished with four Wembley riders, Van Praag, Gregory, Price and Wilks going through to the next round. Once again Van Praag spent hours in his workshop working on a new machine in an attempt to try and regain his world title.

In spite of the lack of enthusiasm shown when Jackson had first tried out midget cars as a second-half attraction, he decided to put on an evening of midget car racing in its own right. Fourteen thousand attended the meeting and this time there was plenty of passing and repassing. The problem was that it left the track in a dreadful state for the Lions' next home meeting against West Ham. One leading member of the team, who wished to remain anonymous, said, 'It's those bally small cars. They tear hell out of any surface. Right down to the foundations they go and it means virtually rebuilding the track after every car meeting if the bikes are to have a fair chance.'

As it happened, the poor state of the track played a large part in Wembley's 48-35 victory. In the second heat, Tiger Stevenson hit a large bump in the track just as he was entering the pit bend. His head shot forward over the handlebars while his teammate, Tommy Croombs, following close behind, swerved to avoid him, falling heavily. Stevenson was carried off to hospital suffering with a bad scalp wound and severe concussion. Although Croombs continued, it was obvious he was still suffering from the effects of the crash, which meant that, effectively, West Ham had lost two of their best riders right at the start of the meeting. Wilkinson was left to battle on almost single-handed for the Hammers, although former Lion Atkinson tried hard. But Wilkinson too suffered from the state of the track, as he crashed in the last heat while leading Van Praag in exactly the same spot as Stevenson. Fortunately, he was not as badly hurt as his colleague, but it turned a 3-3 into a 5-1 for the Lions.

Wembley had mixed fortunes in their next two away matches, losing narrowly at Belle Vue 43-41 but beating Bristol convincingly 50-32. In the latter match Craven played a big part, being his side's top scorer with 10 paid 11. By now, all three of the youngsters were riding so well that they had all made the team proper, with Gregory and Kilmister now at reserve.

Unfortunately from the Lions' point of view, their next meeting with Wimbledon was not the close-run affair all the others had been, as they went down 47-36 at Plough Lane. The encouraging news, however, was that once again Craven was his team's top scorer. The nineteen-year-old Craven's increase in earnings had enabled him to buy a new car, but it broke down so often that he spent more time under it than in it. None of the other riders ever accepted his offer of a lift as they felt it was usually quicker and cheaper to take a bus to wherever they were going.

There was a sensation in Wembley's next home league match against Belle Vue. Van Praag won his first three races but then lost in his last heat to the Aces' Bill Kitchen. It was the first race Van Praag had lost at home in the league all season. Until then he had raced twenty-seven races and won them all. It was Kitchen who scored the maximum this time, but to no avail for his team, as the Lions beat the Aces 47-36. Kitchen's form on the Wembley track was something Jackson took careful note of, hoping one day to be able to put that knowledge to good use.

Wembley's next match was the first leg of the National Trophy semi-final away at Second Division Norwich. Norwich had caused a sensation in the first round by beating First Division Harringay, the first time a lower division team had ever beaten a First Division team in the National Trophy. Once again, Norwich put up a spirited fight, going down by just two points,

George Wilks.

55-53. Their manager and star rider, the former Belle Vue Ace Max Grosskreutz, scored a maximum 18 points and was in a class of his own; even Van Praag trailed badly in his wake. In fact, the only rider to put up any sort of race against him was the Lions' top scorer Wilks, who had probably his best night so far in Wembley colours. After the meeting Van Praag complained of a pain in his leg every time he went out to race. Subsequent X-rays showed that he had a badly pulled thigh muscle. With the World Championship approaching he started on a daily course of violet-ray treatment under the expert hands of Husbands.

Wembley's hopes of regaining the league title all but disappeared in their next match against Harringay, as they went down 47-37, leaving New Cross with a commanding lead. Van Praag, still suffering from his pulled muscle, could only score 8 points. Wilks also scored 8. Charles had a very poor night, contributing just 5.

Wembley's only chance now lay in the next two matches, which were the home and away ties against New Cross. Victory in both of them might just put them back in contention. A loss in just one would mean their league season was over.

The first match was at New Cross on 24 August. It was a hard-fought match and the young trio of Price, Wilks and Craven performed well but, with Van Praag still suffering from his leg injury and Charles seemingly a bit out of touch, it never looked likely that the Lions would be good enough to defeat the Rangers and they went down 45-39.

The following evening saw much the same story as Van Praag, invincible around the Empire Stadium only a few weeks before, could manage only 7 points. Wembley's unlikely hero was Parkinson, who scored a reserve's maximum, but it was not good enough and New Cross to all intents and purposes clinched the league title with a 48-35 victory. They now had 26 points from 17 matches while Wembley, in second place in the league, had 21 from 20. There were

24 matches in a season, so mathematically Wembley could still win, but it would mean New Cross picking up just 2 points from their remaining 7 matches.

Until the last three losses, Wembley were still in with a chance of the title, but the injury to Van Praag's leg and the loss of form of Charles had left them without a rider who could take on and beat the opposition's top riders. Van Praag's injury seemed to be more serious than at first thought and doctors advised him to have a complete rest from speedway. He was told that every time he rode he was aggravating the injury and not giving it time to heal. Van Praag had two problems with this advice. The first was that he was a very loyal team captain and felt his team needed him, even at reduced power. The second was that the World Championship final was coming up and he was determined to win his crown back.

The second half of the home match against New Cross saw Wembley take on Norwich in the second leg of their National Trophy semi-final. Run over just nine heats, Wembley crushed Second Division Norwich 38-15 to win on aggregate 93-68 and progress to the final. Perhaps something could be salvaged from the season after all.

A crowd of 93,000 turned out to see the World final at the Empire Stadium on 1 September. Two Wembley riders qualified for the final – Van Praag and, somewhat surprisingly, Price. Wilkinson had qualified with top bonus points, 8, while Van Praag, Jack Milne, Cordy Milne and Wilbur Lamoreaux all had 7. These five were reckoned to be the favourites to take the title, though much concern was expressed about Van Praag's leg injury. In the end justice was done for Wilkinson, as he took the title from Jack Milne and Lamoreaux. Van Praag did well to finish in fourth place with 11 points on the night and 18 overall. Considering the company he was in, Price rode well for his 4 points on the night, even beating Atkinson and one of the favourites Cordy Milne in one race. A good performance in the World Championship final was a sign of things to come for the young Price.

As well as the National Trophy, Wembley were still in with a chance to add the London Cup to their trophy cabinet. The first leg of their first round match resulted in a 59-49 defeat at the hands of Harringay. Once again Charles was completely off the pace, though Van Praag rode well for his 16 points.

Ten points to make up at home was not out of the reach of the Lions and it looked like the makings of an exciting second leg. Just how exciting was not quite foreseen however. After a first heat finishing 3-3, the Tigers added to their lead with a 5-1 in the second race, putting Wembley 14 points behind. The Lions gradually scraped their way back into the match, but with just four heats to go they were still 6 points down on aggregate. Heat fifteen saw a 5-1 to Charles and Craven, putting them 2 behind. In heat sixteen, Case proved to be the only finisher, so a 3-0 to Wembley gave them a one-point advantage. With the scores still so close and the final result still anyone's guess, heat seventeen proved to be one of the most controversial ever witnessed at the Empire Stadium.

In the first attempt to complete the race, Harringay's Norman Parker fell, bringing down his teammate Lloyd Goffe with him. The steward immediately stopped the race and ordered a re-run without Parker. In the re-run, Goffe led until the last bend where Craven ran into him, knocking him from his machine. Craven's exclusion light came on and he was disqualified for boring but, crucially, the steward allowed the race to continue, leaving Price to finish alone. Goffe eventually picked himself up and pushed his bike across the finishing line, where he promptly collapsed and was carried off. The result was a 3-2 to Wembley. Harringay immediately protested that the race should have been re-run as, by allowing it to go on, Goffe, the innocent victim of Craven's boring, had lost his chance to win the race. As Goffe was in the lead at the time of the incident they argued that Craven's foul had benefited his team and the result should not be allowed to stand. The steward dismissed their protest and Harringay now found themselves two points behind going into the final race. As it happened, Van Praag and Charles made no mistake in that final race, romping home to a 5-1 to give Wembley the leg 60-44 and the tie 109-103.

Apart from the heat seventeen incident, Wembley had much to celebrate, as Van Praag was right back on top form with a maximum 18 points. Charles too was much improved, scoring 9 along with Price.

Wembley were through to the second round of the London Cup and now faced a sequence of four matches against Wimbledon. The first at Plough Lane was the first leg of the London Cup semi-final; the second at Wembley was the first leg of the National Trophy final; the third at Wimbledon was the second leg of the National Trophy final and the fourth and last at the Empire Stadium was the second leg of the London Cup semi-final. Unfortunately for the Lions Wimbledon cleaned up, winning all four matches, leaving Wembley once again without a single trophy to show for their season's hard work.

Wembley ended the season winning three out of their last four league matches, including two wins in their last home meeting of the season, a double header against Wimbledon and Harringay. In the end they finished the league in third place, having just been pipped to the runner-up spot by West Ham on race points difference. Van Praag finished the season in fourth place overall in the averages with 10.50, a good performance considering the problems he had with his leg towards the end of the season. Charles's form had dipped during the year and he finished with an average of 8.48. But most encouraging for the Lions and for their prospects the following season was the form shown by their three youngsters, all of whom finished with averages of over 6 points per match. Craven finished with an average of 6.99, Wilks with 6.91 and Price with 6.07.

1938 National League Averages – qualification 6 matches

	Matches	Rides	Points	BP	Total	CMA
Lionel Van Praag	22	88	225	6	231	10.50
Frank Charles	23	92	186	9	195	8.48
Malcolm Craven	23	79	117	21	138	6.99
George Wilks	24	92	148	11	159	6.91
Cliff Parkinson	19	54	76	12	88	6.52
Tommy Price	24	89	114	21	135	6.07
Dicky Case	13	41	48	13	61	5.95
Eric Gregory	21	77	75	19	94	4.88
Wally Kilmister	20	53	48	14	62	4.68

National League Matches

Date	H/A	Against	W/L/D	Score
29 April	Away	Bristol	Won	47-37
4 May	Away	New Cross	Lost	39-45
12 May	Home	Belle Vue	Won	54-30
14 May	Away	Belle Vue	Lost	36-48
17 May	Away	West Ham	Lost	34-40
19 May	Home	West Ham	Won	44-40
23 May	Away	Wimbledon	Drew	42-42
26 May	Home	Wimbledon	Won	43-41
2 June	Home	New Cross	Lost	37-46
4 June	Away	Harringay	Won	45-38
30 June	Home	Harringay	Won	50-34
21 July	Home	West Ham	Won	48-35
28 July	Home	Bristol	Won	57-27
29 July	Away	Bristol	Won	50-32
30 July	Away	Belle Vue	Lost	41-43
1 August	Away	Wimbledon	Lost	36-47
4 August	Home	Belle Vue	Won	47-36
13 August	Away	Harringay	Lost	37-47
24 August	Away	New Cross	Lost	39-45
25 August	Home	New Cross	Lost	35-48
22 September	Home	Harringay	Won	49-35
4 October	Away	West Ham	Lost	34-50
6 October	Home	Wimbledon	Won	45-39
6 October	Home	Harringay	Won	54-28

National League Table

	Played	Won	Drawn	Lost	For	Against	Points
New Cross	24	15	1	8	1,072	925	31
West Ham	24	13	1	10	1,050.5	939.5	27
WEMBLEY	24	13	1	10	1,043	953	27
Wimbledon	24	12	3	9	1,005	996	27
Belle Vue	24	11	0	13	949	1,052	22
Harringay	24	10	1	13	980	1,018	21
Bristol	24	6	1	17	890.5	1,106.5	13

National Trophy

Quarter-Final
Wembley 61 Belle Vue 47
Belle Vue 60 Wembley 48
Aggregate: Wembley 109 Belle Vue 107

Semi-Final
Wembley 38 Norwich 15
Norwich 53 Wembley 55
Aggregate: Wembley 93 Norwich 68

Final
Wimbledon 58 Wembley 49
Wembley 43 Wimbledon 65
Aggregate: Wimbledon 123 Wembley 92

ACU Cup

Pool Two
Wembley 67 Belle Vue 40
Wembley 61 Bristol 47
Wembley 54 Wimbledon 54
Belle Vue 71 Wembley 36
Bristol 44 Wembley 64
Wimbledon 54 Wembley 53

Race Points
Wimbledon 355
Wembley 335
Belle Vue 320
Bristol 283

London Cup

First Round
Wembley 60 Harringay 44
Harringay 59 Wembley 49
Aggregate: Wembley 109 Harringay 103

Semi-Final
Wimbledon 66 Wembley 42
Wembley 47 Wimbledon 61
Aggregate: Wimbledon 127 Wembley 89

English Speedway Trophy (Southern Section) matches

Wembley Reserves 52 Birmingham 32
Wembley Reserves 24 Hackney Wick 58
Wembley Reserves 49 New Cross Reserves 34
Wembley Reserves 36 Norwich 48
Wembley Reserves 33 Southampton 48
Birmingham 46 Wembley Reserves 36
Hackney Wick 54 Wembley Reserves 30
New Cross Reserves 52 Wembley Reserves 30
Norwich 40 Wembley Reserves 44
Southampton 53 Wembley Reserves 29

English Speedway Trophy (Southern Section) Table

	Played	Won	Drawn	Lost	For	Against	Points
Southampton	10	9	0	1	512	311	18
Hackney Wick	10	6	0	4	442	386	12
Norwich	10	6	0	4	397	435	12
Birmingham	10	5	0	5	430	401	10
WEMBLEY RESERVES	10	3	0	7	363	465	6
New Cross Reserves	10	1	0	9	338	484	2

TWELVE

1939 – WE'LL NEVER KNOW

A number of alterations were made to the track and stadium during the close season. The bends were relaid and special drainage put in to prevent water-logging in the case of a heavy downpour. The stand accommodation was considerably improved – all the wooden stands were replaced by concrete, allowing spectators to stand nearer the track. Track lighting, which was already the best in the country, was more than doubled.

On the rider front, a new Australian by the name of Lawson was signed up on the recommendation of Van Praag, who said he was 'the best rider to come out of Australia for seven years.' His christian name was initially given as Albert though it was, in fact, Aubrey. However, he was soon to be universally known as Aub. In addition the Dane Morian Hansen was transferred from Bristol.

To offset the arrival of Lawson and Hansen there were a number of departures. Watson finally transferred officially to West Ham, Charles decided to retire so he could concentrate on his gliding – he told Jackson he was still determined to break that gliding record – and Case, though he said he was still available in emergencies, told Jackson that he wanted to concentrate on his Rye House school.

The Wembley team for 1939 was therefore announced as Van Praag (captain), Craven, Wilks, Price, Gregory, Parkinson, Menzies, Wells, Kilmister, Lawson and Hansen. Three new youngsters were also taken under Jackson's wing: Frank Woodroffe, an Australian, Fred Belliveau, a Canadian and Jack Peck. In the event, Kilmister too decided it was time to retire, thus severing his link with Wembley, which went back to 1930.

Van Praag had spent the winter racing in Australia. On his return he complained that his leg injury was still giving him trouble and that the torn muscles in the groin had still not healed properly. He said he could run and jump without any problem but when he dragged his foot through a cinder bump he still got a nasty twinge.

With the idea of adding to the spectacle of racing, all the Wembley machines were chromium plated. A new compressed-air washing plant was installed in the workshops to make sure the bikes remained clean.

Once again there was a small change to the National League line-up as Southampton replaced Bristol.

Wembley lost the chance of winning one trophy in 1939 before the season even started, as it was announced that a new competition, the British Speedway Cup, would replace the ACU Cup. The

Aub Lawson.

drawback for Wembley was the matches were to be raced at the beginning of the season before the Empire Stadium was ready to stage speedway. Although they offered to race away matches only with double points at stake, or to use Hackney as a temporary home, both of these proposals were turned down by the control board and they had no option but to withdraw.

The opening event of the speedway season, an individual event called the Rangers' Cup, took place at New Cross on 29 March. It was won by Price with Wilks taking third place. With Craven also riding well in the event, things looked good for the Lions for 1939.

Wembley's first match of the season was a challenge, away to Second Division Newcastle, which the Lions had no difficulty in winning 54-28. Lawson made his debut, but could only score 2 points. Both Craven and Wilks scored maximums, while Price dropped just one point.

Unfortunately, because Wembley were not taking part in the British Speedway Cup, this was their only outing as a team until 11 May, their official opening date. The only competitive riding experience the team members were getting was in second-half bookings. Naturally Van Praag was picking up the most, but even he reckoned he only earned about £30 in total for the first part of the season. The others were lucky if they received half of that. Jackson was concerned about the lack of riding on the part of his team, firstly because it meant all the other teams were getting fit and back in to the swing of riding, getting used to the tracks and so on, and secondly because he was unable to see how his riders were shaping up and who to put in the team and in what riding order.

For the opening league meeting at the Empire Stadium against Wimbledon on 11 May, Jackson went with Van Praag/Gregory; Price/Hansen; Wilks/Craven with Parkinson and Wells at reserve for his line-up. Although the Lions won the match comfortably, in spite of their lack of racing, by 53 points to 30, there was a disaster in the very first heat as Gregory fell and broke his right arm. He told reporters, 'Just my luck, but never mind, I'll be riding again in maybe six weeks' time.' For Jackson, in the meantime, it meant having to re-order his team. Van Praag opened the season with a maximum, while Craven gave strong support with 10.

Jackson decided to move Parkinson up into the team to replace Gregory and to bring Lawson in as reserve. He also decided to replace Wells with Menzies.

The importation of Lawson into the team brought with it a problem. Before the injury to Gregory, Jackson had decided to give Lawson more experience by loaning him to Second Division Middlesbrough. As it was felt at this stage that Gregory would only be out for a few weeks, agreement was reached with Middlesbrough and the control board that Lawson could ride for both clubs until the end of May. On 26 May Lawson was due to ride for Middlesbrough in a National Trophy first round match. According to the rules no rider was allowed to turn out for two teams in the National Trophy. Jackson felt an exception should be made in Lawson's case and appealed to the control board. As he put it, 'If he [Lawson] is barred from helping Wembley in the National Trophy later on, we will be penalised for helping Middlesbrough, who have been allowed to use Lawson without any charge.' The *Speedway News* hoped that if Jackson's appeal to the control board was successful that Middlesbrough would not be drawn to meet Wembley in a later round, as Lawson might finish up riding against himself!

Lawson showed his worth in the next match as he scored a paid reserve's maximum in the exciting 45-45 home draw with Harringay. The score, with two heats to go, was Wembley 35 Harringay 37. The line-up for the penultimate heat was Hansen and Lawson for the Lions, Alec Statham and Frank Dolan for the Tigers. As the tapes went up, Statham sailed off into a commanding lead with his partner, Dolan, holding second place. To the Wembley faithful it looked all over. A 5-1 to Harringay would give them an unassailable lead to take into the last heat. But Statham made a fatal blunder. He slowed to allow Dolan to catch up so they could team ride. But, like a bolt from the blue, Lawson suddenly flashed past from nowhere to take the lead. The crowd gasped in amazement then shouted in sheer exultation as Dolan fell. As the race went on Lawson increased his lead and never looked like being caught. A certain 5-1 to Harringay had turned into a 4-2 for Wembley, thanks to the young Australian sensation. Van Praag scored his usual maximum while good support came from Wilks and Price.

With Lawson showing such promising form, Jackson chose him to accompany Van Praag as the Wembley entry for the National League Best Pairs Competition. The contest was held at Belle Vue and, after the scheduled sixteen heats, the Lions' pair lay in joint-first place with West Ham. They had scored a total of 17 points, Van Praag getting 11 and Lawson 6. A run-off for the title was held against the Hammers' pairing of Arthur Atkinson and Tommy Croombs, and it was Lawson who proved to be the Wembley hero, as he took first place. With Van Praag coming in third, it was a victory for the Lions' pair.

Wembley's next home match resulted in a big win against New Cross, 52-31. Wells was back at reserve. Van Praag's maximum was given solid support by his young team members, Wilks scored 8, Craven and Lawson 7 and Price 6. With Hansen also weighing in with 8, it seemed that Wembley had a very strong team that was going to be very hard to beat. Jackson, his team and supporters now dared to think that perhaps this year they would at last see the return of that National League title. The only cautionary note to the optimism in the Wembley camp was that they had yet to ride an away fixture.

It was just after this match that it became apparent that Gregory's injury was far worse than at first realised. Not only had he fractured a bone but he had crushed a nerve in the accident. A successful operation raised the nerve and carefully placed it back in position, but doctors were now talking about three or more months before he would be fit to ride again. Sadly, as it transpired, Gregory was never able to return to the saddle. It was an unhappy end for such a Wembley stalwart.

The first away fixture on 29 May promptly punctured the Wembley euphoria that had set in over the last few matches, as the Lions went down to a heavy defeat, 51-33, at the hands of Wimbledon. Lawson, promoted to the team proper for the first time at the expense of Parkinson, managed 5 points, including a 5-1 last-heat win with Craven but, apart from his contribution, the younger element did not live up to expectations and it was left to Van Praag once again to put up any sort of fight as he netted 10 points.

The next match, at home, saw the Lions back to winning ways with a comprehensive 50-34 victory over Belle Vue. Strangely, this time Lawson was the only one of the younger riders who did not do well, scoring just 2, while Craven with 11, Price with 9 and Wilks with 7 provided match-winning backing to Van Praag's 11.

Van Praag had an unfortunate start to the London Riders' Championship, missing his first ride due to late arrival. On his way to New Cross he had gone through a red light and was pulled up by the police. He told the policeman who he was and why he was in a hurry and offered to leave his documents with him and pick them up from the police station after the meeting, but the police constable was having none of it and insisted on looking through his licence and insurance there and then. By the time Van Praag made it to the Old Kent Road, he had missed his first ride. Worse still, in his second programmed ride his motor packed up. He finished in seventh place with 7 points. Price was the highest-placed Wembley rider with 8 points.

Wembley's next league match was at West Ham. But it was no ordinary match as the West Ham and former Wembley promoter Johnnie Hoskins had turned it into a Royal occasion by inviting HRH the Duchess of Kent. The occasion seemed to inspire the Lions as they ran out winners 48-36. It was the first home match West Ham had lost this season and the result was largely due to the fact that the whole of the Wembley team made their presence felt. Even Menzies, who had not had a good season up to then, won a race, beating old-time Lions favourites Colin Watson and Phil Bishop in one race.

Three Wembley riders were chosen for their respective teams in the first Test at New Cross. Van Praag captained Australia, who also included Lawson at reserve, while Price turned out at reserve for England. It was a measure of how far these young riders had come that they were now being chosen to represent their countries.

Having only lost one match, Wembley were well on course for the league title with their young team. But no-one, not even Jackson, was prepared for the next boost to their chances. While the next home match, against West Ham, was in progress, Frank Charles walked into the pits and told Jackson that he wanted to ride again. 'Seems that I can't get the cinders out of my system,' he said. 'For several months I've been acting as gliding instructor to a bunch of Air Defence Cadets at Barrow-in-Furness. Though the work's interesting, life's been very slow and I've missed the roar of racing machines.'

Although Jackson was pleased to have Charles back it raised two problems for him. The first was what would happen to Hansen, who was allocated to Wembley because of Charles's retirement. The second was that Jackson did not want to upset the balance of his team, which was going so well at the moment. He decided that, if Hansen was to be allowed to stay, Charles would have to start off at reserve in place of Menzies. Although, of course, Jackson expected Charles to score far more points than Menzies, he was reluctant to let him go as he had made a rapid improvement since finding a place in the team, especially since Henry Richards, one of the Wembley mechanics, had built a special frame for him. Nevertheless, with the very real possibility of the league title coming their way, Jackson decided he had no option and agreed to loan out Menzies to a Second Division club for the remainder of the season.

The Lions' next match was in the London Cup, the semi-final first leg at home to Wimbledon. As soon as the news of Charles's return to Wembley was announced, the Wimbledon management put in a protest to the control board about Wembley being allowed to keep Hansen. The control board asked Wimbledon to quote the regulation under which their protest was being made. By the time of the match, Wimbledon had not responded but they felt nonetheless that the control board should not allow Charles to race until the matter was resolved, and raced the match under protest. Jackson's comment on the situation was that he had no intention of letting any of his present riders go. He added that if any track wanted to sign Charles themselves they would have to pay a transfer fee of £1,000, and then it would be up to Charles whether he wanted to go or not. 'It has taken us a long time to build up the present Wembley team,' he said, 'and during that building-up process we did not ask or look for assistance from other clubs. Wimbledon imply they are weak. This is not in accordance with their present league status, for they have yet to be beaten at home and have lost only one away league match. I would like to remind Wimbledon that they have had the pick of American riders, while only last season they secured the transfer from Bristol of Vic Duggan, who was top point scorer for Australia in the recent Test match.'

Jackson then took a swipe at New Cross whose promoter, Freddie Mockford, had also objected and had asked for the control board to allocate either Hansen or Charles to them. 'If New Cross feel they need strengthening,' Jackson said, 'then they made a rather puzzling move by allowing Ernie Evans to go to Sheffield as he was showing good form at the time.' He finished his tirade against fellow promoters with a defence of his actions, in particular his youth policy. 'When Hackney put their riders on the market all clubs had the opportunity of securing these riders. I obtained Wilks and Case, but no effort was made by other clubs to secure these riders. Now that Wembley's patience in coaching youngsters is bearing fruit some people are bemoaning that Wembley are too strong. Wembley took a gamble by bringing Aub Lawson over from Australia, for he is young and his Australian record was not strong enough to indicate his recent amazing jump to stardom. In speedway racing one has to take chances and not depend on the energy of others for riders.'

After all that, Wimbledon proved to be the strongest of the two by knocking Wembley out of the London Cup, losing by just three points, 55-52, at the Empire Stadium, and then beating them back at Plough Lane by ten points, 59-49, to take the semi-final 111-104. In spite of losing, Wembley were more than pleased with the showing of Charles in his first match back, as he scored 10 points from four races at reserve to be second highest scorer behind Van Praag's eighteen-point maximum. Price also scored 10. Ironically, in view of the ongoing protest by Wimbledon, the top two Lions scorers at Plough Lane were Hansen with 12 and Charles with 10. Van Praag had a very poor evening, contributing just 6 to the Wembley total. Opinion throughout the country now was that the league title was between these two teams as they had shown themselves to be equally matched and far above any other side.

Like Charles, it was now Kilmister's turn to tell Jackson that he would like to make a comeback. Given Kilmister's form over the last couple of years, however, Jackson could not find a spot in the team for him and loaned him out to Southampton instead.

Wembley's strength was confirmed when they crushed Southampton 57-27 on 22 June. Three riders reached double figures: Van Praag with 11 paid 12 and Hansen and Wilks with 10 each.

Morian Hansen.

Two days later, however, Wembley were on the receiving end of a similar scoreline to the team that had so often proved their nemesis in the past. Many people thought that Belle Vue's best years were behind them, but no-one had told Belle Vue. Only Van Praag and, to a lesser extent, Charles, could match the Aces' big guns of Langton, Varey, Kitchen and Abbott. Craven was third-highest Wembley scorer with 3. Menzies returned at reserve for this match in place of Parkinson.

Four days later came an even bigger blow to Wembley's hopes as they lost to league newcomers Southampton 46-38. This time it was Van Praag and Hansen who put up the fight, but even they were no match for the flying Cordy Milne.

Another defeat at home followed, this time to Wimbledon. Wembley's chances of that league title, which only three matches before had seemed distinctly rosy now looked like a bit of an uphill struggle.

When the averages up to the end of June were published, only Van Praag from Wembley figured in the top twelve. With an average of 10.33, he was in fifth place. Cordy Milne was well in the lead with 11.20.

For a team that had promised so much at the beginning of the season, with probably the strongest sextet in the league, things were going badly wrong. When asked why this was, Jackson replied that all riders have bad patches and he cited Bill Longley at New Cross, Geoff Pymar at Wimbledon and Joe Abbott at Belle Vue. 'But,' he continued, 'Wembley are going through the unique experience of having at least four riders go stale at the same time. It's a worrying time. Van Praag and Charles are going marvellously, but how can two men carry a team? Yet I know I've got the best, the happiest and the most easily managed fellows in the sport. Don't think there's anything wrong in the den – there isn't, except just a severe epidemic of staleness for which, I tell myself every day, the cure must come. See how hard Morian is trying. Look how Tommy Price is fighting his hay fever. George Wilks has taken quite a few useful points lately and the medicine is having much effect. Malcolm Craven's only trouble is that he takes himself too seriously. Two or three performances earlier on have got Malcolm down. He needs to regain his self-confidence. It'll come. I haven't lost the opinion, which I have frequently aired, that in

Malcolm I've got the best youngster the game has seen for many seasons. All Wembley needs is time to shake off the staleness. It is going gradually. But it is a difficult thing to combat. There's nothing wrong with Wembley. Barring poor Eric Gregory, we've dodged serious injury, for which I'm very thankful. Watch us fight to the top from today onwards and see if I'm not right when I say that in a month's time the parrot-cry will be 'Wembley's too strong.'

The very next match after this optimistic view of his team's chances saw a delighted Jackson as the Lions trounced West Ham 58-26. As predicted, the whole team seemed to come good at once, with Van Praag and Charles leading the way. Their tally of 11 each was backed up with 10 from Wilks, 8 from Craven and 6 each from Hansen and Price. And to prove this was no fluke, two days later Wembley defeated Harringay at Green Lanes by 48 to 36. Van Praag scored his fifth maximum of the season, while Price supported with 10 and Charles, Craven and Lawson with 7 each.

Their next encounter was the two-leg National Trophy first round tie against West Ham. West Ham won the first leg 62-46. Van Praag lost just once, to Atkinson, and received good backing from Wilks and Lawson with 8 each, but Charles seemed to be out of sorts, scoring just 3, while Hansen failed to score at all.

Wembley fought hard in the return leg at the Empire Stadium to cut down the sixteen-point deficit and, with one heat to go, Wembley had just managed to take a two-point overall lead, so it was still anyone's tie. And what an epic heat eighteen turned out to be! Van Praag rode a true captain's race as though his life depended on it. He managed to get to the first bend just in front and maintained the lead going into the back straight, with Atkinson just inches behind. Tommy Croombs was tearing along in third place but Craven was completely tailed off. Van Praag realised that the whole outcome of the tie depended on him. Atkinson pushed him all the way in a battle between two masters of the speedway. The crowd were yelling themselves hoarse as the riders swung into the last lap side by side, Van Praag hugging the white line with Atkinson roaring round the outside. As they rounded the first bend, Atkinson wobbled slightly and this was enough to give Van Praag a slight breathing space and he reached the last bend just in front. He held his lead round the final bend and crossed the winning line less than two lengths to the good, but enough to give Wembley the tie. They were through to the National Trophy second round and their sights were still set on the double. But this was to be Charles's last match.

Just as things were beginning to look up for the Lions, tragedy struck. While competing in the National Gliding Competition at Great Hucklow in Derbyshire on 15 July, Frank Charles's glider crashed from a height of 300 feet. He was killed instantly.

Wembley's next match against Harringay was cancelled but the Lions were back in action on 27 July. Craven was promoted to heat leader, Lawson was promoted to the team proper and Menzies was brought back from loan to Stoke to take up one of the reserve positions again. So the line-up now was Van Praag/Lawson; Craven/Hansen; Price/Wilks with Menzies and Parkinson at reserve.

The first match without Charles was a tight squeeze, but the Lions just managed it as they defeated Belle Vue 43-41. Craven lived up to his new heat leader status by being Wembley's top scorer in the match with 10 points, equal to Van Praag. He scored another 10 in the next match, a 61-23 demolition of Southampton. Craven seemed to relish his new role and was looking the best of Jackson's crop of discoveries. He had now joined Van Praag in the league's top twelve point scorers with an average of 7.00. Van Praag had 10.47 and was now in fourth place behind Cordy Milne (11.23), Wilbur Lamoreaux (10.85) and Vic Duggan (10.53).

Wembley's resurgence was halted with two away losses, the first at Wimbledon, 44-40, and the second at West Ham, 53-31. It now looked all over for Wembley's chances of taking the league title, which was rapidly coming down to a contest between Belle Vue and Wimbledon. As events transpired, Wembley had just one more league match to race, a home fixture against New Cross, which they won 59-24 with all three heat leaders, Van Praag, Craven and Price, scoring maximums and Hansen adding a paid maximum.

Because of his recent good form, Craven was chosen to represent England in the fifth Test at Wembley. Price was also chosen, as was Wilks at reserve. Van Praag was captain of Australia and Lawson rode as his partner. Altogether, five of the six Wembley team members were chosen; the other team member was Danish, of course. The result was a big win for England, 71-36, with Craven contributing 11 and Price 9. For Australia Van Praag was top scorer with 11, while Lawson got 5.

Heat seven of the match was an-all Wembley heat as Craven and Price took on Van Praag and Lawson. Unexpectedly it was won by Lawson, with Craven edging Van Praag out of second place.

Wembley's last two competitive matches before the Second World War were the two National Trophy semi-final legs against Southampton. In a sign of what was about to happen, Jackson was unable to be present for these ties, as he had been called up for duty and given the rank of Captain. Southampton made more of a match of it than many people expected by winning the first leg 62-46. Back at the Empire Stadium, however, it was a different story as the Lions thrashed the Saints 74-33, winning 120-95 on aggregate and going through to the National Trophy final for the second year running, where they were due to meet the old enemy Belle Vue.

After the match itself two scratch races were held, with the second one being the Champions' Scratch Race between Van Praag, Jack Milne, Wilbur Lamoreaux and Cordy Milne. It was won by Van Praag, who was therefore the last rider to win a race at the Empire Stadium before war broke out, and with Lamoreaux coming last he became the last rider to cross the line.

At the end of that final season, Van Praag finished fifth in the averages with a cma of 10.61. Craven's late run since being given the responsibility of heat leader saw him shoot up the averages to finish in twelfth place with 8.32.

The following week, on 7 September, the 1939 World Championship final was due to be held. Cordy Milne, who was having a tremendous season, was top qualifier, taking 8 bonus points with him. Two Wembley riders qualified for the final, Van Praag with 6 bonus points and Lawson with 4. Craven was the top non-qualifier and was therefore due to be first reserve. A record crowd was expected and the 106,000-capacity stadium was likely to be sold out. In May, 100,000 had seen the FA Cup final, but the seats on the popular terraces on that occasion had been removed, making room for about 6,000 more spectators.

But the final was never held as war was declared on 3 September and all sporting events suspended. Although some other tracks were able to put on limited wartime racing, most notably Belle Vue, Wembley had seen its last activity on the track for the duration.

It was to be a long seven years for the Wembley faithful but the foundations of the team that was to take British speedway by storm in the late 1940s and early 1950s had been laid by Jackson, and its story will be told in part two of the history of Wembley speedway – 'The Post-War Years'.

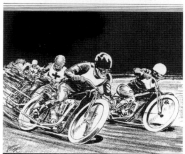

The programme cover from the last meeting at Wembley before the Second World War, a National Trophy semi-final match against Southampton on 31 August 1939.

1939 National League Averages – qualification 6 matches

	Matches	Rides	Points	BP	Total	CMA
Lionel Van Praag	19	75	198	1	199	10.61
Malcolm Craven	19	76	140	18	158	8.32
Frank Charles	7	26	47	6	53	8.15
Tommy Price	19	74	125	15	140	7.57
Morian Hansen	19	72	108	21	129	7.17
George Wilks	19	76	110	18	128	6.74
Aub Lawson	18	61	75	12	87	5.70
Cliff Parkinson	18	41	44	8	52	5.07
Andy Menzies	11	24	20	5	25	4.17

National League Matches

Date	H/A	Against	W/L/D	Score
11 May	Home	Wimbledon	Won	53-30
18 May	Home	Harringay	Drew	42-42
25 May	Home	New Cross	Won	52-31
29 May	Away	Wimbledon	Lost	33-51
1 June	Home	Belle Vue	Won	50-34
6 June	Away	West Ham	Won	48-36
8 June	Home	West Ham	Won	55-29
21 June	Away	New Cross	Lost	40-42
22 June	Home	Southampton	Won	57-27
24 June	Away	Belle Vue	Lost	27-57
28 June	Away	Southampton	Lost	38-46
29 June	Home	Wimbledon	Lost	39-45

6 July	Home	West Ham	Won	58-26
8 July	Away	Harringay	Won	48-36
27 July	Home	Belle Vue	Won	43-41
3 August	Home	Southampton	Won	61-22
7 August	Away	Wimbledon	Lost	40-44
8 August	Away	West Ham	Lost	31-53
10 August	Home	New Cross	Won	59-24

National League Table as at 3 September on the suspension of speedway

	Played	Won	Drawn	Lost	For	Against	Points
Belle Vue	16	12	1	3	762	575	25
Wimbledon	18	12	0	6	807	695	24
WEMBLEY	19	11	1	7	874	716	23
West Ham	19	9	0	10	766	819	18
Harringay	16	7	1	8	662	674	15
Southampton	17	5	0	12	611.5	811.5	10
New Cross	19	4	1	14	695.5	887.5	9

National Trophy

Quarter-Final
Wembley 63 West Ham 45
West Ham 62 Wembley 46
Aggregate: Wembley 109 West Ham 107

Semi-Final
Wembley 74 Southampton 33
Southampton 62 Wembley 46
Aggregate: Wembley 120 Southampton 95

Final
Wembley v. Belle Vue
Not held owing to suspension of speedway

London Cup

First Round
Wembley: Bye

Semi-Final
Wimbledon 59 Wembley 49
Wembley 55 Wimbledon 52
Aggregate: Wimbledon 111 Wembley 104

APPENDICES

Appendix 1 – List of Contracted Pre-War Wembley Riders

Atkinson, Arthur	1929-30	Kirkman, Ken	1934
Balliol, Carl	1930	Kuhn, Gus	1937-38
Barrett, Charlie	1929-30	Lamont, Billy	1935-37
Belliveau, Fred	1939	Lawson, Aub	1939
Brown, A.	1930	Lees, H.R. (Ginger)	1932-37
Bounds, Reg	1932-34	Little, Wally	1934; 1937
Bowden, Les	1934-38	Lloyd, Jeff	1938
Briggs, Charlie	1929	Lloyd, Wally	1936-37
Byers, Gordon	1932-36	Menzies, Andy	1938-39
Case, Dicky	1938	Millward, Jack	1934-37
Catlett, Stan	1929-31	Mordue, Gus	1930
Charles, Frank	1935-39	Ormston, Jack	1929-32
Chick, Alf	1929	Parkinson, Cliff	1930-33; 1936-39
Craven, Malcolm	1937-39	Peck, Jack	1939
de la Porte, Cecil	1936-37	Pidcock, Tom	1930
Deale, Vic	1929	Price, Tommy	1935-39
Dixon, Jack 'Bronco'	1934-35	Reeve, Len	1929-30
Dunn, Percy	1933	Rous, Crawley	1929
Evans, Norman	1930-33; 1935	Shelton, Charlie	1930-32
Fairweather, Bert	1929-30	Smythe, Dicky	1935
Frogley, Buster	1929-31	Stewart, Col	1931-32
Frogley, Roger	1936	Sticpewich, Bill	1929-30
George Greenwood	1930-32; 1934-37	Stobart, Maurice	1933
Gregory, Eric	1934-39	Tauser, Ray	1929
Hannaford, George	1935	Taylor, Ray	1935
Hansen, Morian	1939	Van Praag, Lionel	1931-39
Herbert, Hal	1933	Warren, Art	1929-30
Hieatt, Burn	1929	Warren, Sam	1938
Hieatt, Ron	1929-30	Watson, Colin	1930-38
Howsley, Fred	1929	Wells, Bob	1938-39
Jackson, Jack	1929-32	White, Terry	1930
Kaines	1938	Whitfield, Harry	1930-38
Key, Nobby	1929	Wilks, George	1938-39
Kilmister, Wally	1930-39	Woodroffe, Frank	1939

Appendix 2 –Top average year by year

1929	Jack Ormston	11.16
1930	Jack Ormston	10.06
1931	Colin Watson	8.88
1932	Ginger Lees	10.25
1933	Wally Kilmister	9.33
1934	Ginger Lees	9.88
1935	Frank Charles	8.70
1936	Frank Charles	10.00
1937	Lionel Van Praag	10.53
1938	Lionel Van Praag	10.50
1939	Lionel Van Praag	10.61

Appendix 3 – Overall Top Scorers 1929-1939

Name	Years	Rides	Pts	CMA
Lionel Van Praag	1931-1939	703	1,449	8.17
Wally Kilmister	1930-1938	571	988.5	6.56
Ginger Lees	1932-1937	446	968	8.37
Frank Charles	1935-1939	370	800	8.65
Colin Watson	1930-1938	385	744	7.46
Gordon Byers	1932-1936	403	626	6.07

Appendix 4 – Four-Lap Standing Start (1929-1932)/Clutch Start (1933-1939) Record

1 Lap = 344 metres (378 yards)

16 May 1928	Bert Fairweather	91.6 seconds
6 June 1929	Drew McQueen	91.2 seconds
13 June 1929	Roger Frogley	90.4 seconds
4 July 1929	Harry Whitfield	90.0 seconds
25 July 1929	Jack Ormston	89.6 seconds
15 August 1929	Charlie Barrett	89.2 seconds
22 August 1929	Gus Kuhn	88.4 seconds
29 August 1929	Arthur Atkinson	88.0 seconds
29 October 1928	Jack Ormston	86.2 seconds
22 May 1930	Vic Huxley	85.4 seconds
By end of 1930	Harry Whitfield	84.8 seconds
30 July 1931	Jack Parker	83.6 seconds
Before 14 July 1932	Reg Bounds	83.6 seconds
18 May 1933	Ginger Lees	79.6 seconds
25 May 1933	Claude Rye	78.6 seconds
28 September 1933	Eric Langton	78.6 seconds
26 October 1933	Frank Charles	78.4 seconds
35 Mat 1934	Frank Pearce	78.2 seconds
7 June 1934	Tom Farndon	77.2 seconds
26 July 1934	Ginger Lees	76.4 seconds
29 August 1935	Max Grosskreutz	76.2 seconds
29 August 1935	Frank Charles	76.2 seconds
28 May 1936	Frank Charles	75.0 seconds
10 September 1936	Frank Charles	73.6 seconds
18 August 1938	Alec Statham	73.4 seconds
15 June 1939	Lionel Van Praag	73.2 seconds